D1561705

# The Human Cougar

# The Human Cougar

## by Lloyd L. Morain

**℞ Prometheus Books**

Buffalo, N.Y. 14215

Published 1976 by Prometheus Books
923 Kensington Avenue, Buffalo, New York 14215


Copyright © by Prometheus Books

Library of Congress Card Number 75-46147
ISBN 0-87975-062-6


Printed in the United States of America

# Contents

# Preface

The Human Cougar is an endangered species. Roaming about, free from regimentation, overlooked by bureaucracies, and largely outside of social welfare systems, he often escapes notice. Yet this outsider is very much a part of American life, and the West as we know it was largely created by this brand of working drifter.

Our heavily institutionalized modern society is inhospitable to the Human Cougar, but there are millions of individuals among us who have a latent Cougar strain. They are independent, hard working, and law-abiding, though they resist authority for authority's sake. They often find it difficult to put heart and soul into any highly structured work or social program. The Protestant ethic and traditional attitudes toward family life may present obstacles to this kind of existence. Those with a Cougar strain can better understand their own inner stirrings by gaining knowledge of the independent hard-living breed now ebbing into extinction.

# Acknowledgments

To the hundreds of Human Cougars who have shared high-lights of their hard and lusty lives with me I offer warm, grateful thanks. In chance meetings on waterfronts and highways, in railyards, hobo jungles, orchards, cattle ranches, mines, logging camps, bars, and coffee shops, Cougars have given me insights into ways of life I could never experience fully.

These Cougars have shown that pleasure and satisfaction in the immediate do not depend upon material possessions or a substantial annual income. Many of the pluses of living cannot be measured in economic terms. Independence and personal dignity are possible, though increasingly difficult, in our highly structured society. In their lifestyles they respect law but not authority that is imposed just because it is authority. One can be civilized without knuckling under to all of the civilizing institutions.

I have been fortunate in being able to explore some of these ideas with Eric Furbish, O. Lloyd Hicks, Eugene Mihailovich, Thomas E. McAnally, Kenneth Hunt, and Don R. Morton. Practical and helpful suggestions for bringing the Cougar species to wider attention have been given by Christina Floyd, Sherley Ashton, and Roger Williams. In particular I am indebted to my wife Mary who for many years has accepted an occasional overnight absence as justifiable on the basis of its being "Cougar business."

# Sighting the Cougar

After a year and a half, and after becoming the saw-mill foreman, I quit my job due to my wife's death and became a tramp. I guess to be fair you could call me a part-time tramp because there have been times through the years that I have had some good-paying jobs, and I would work mostly at these jobs in the winter seasons. Sometimes I worked in Nevada, Idaho, and Arizona on horse and cattle ranches, other times as a heavy equipment operator on construction work.

But when summer came, it was like a magnetic force pulling me back to the road. I can't explain it, but it seemed to be I was trying to go back into the past rather than go forward into the future. It appeared that I had been looking for some unattainable thing or some unattainable someone. I always had the feeling of "maybe," but "maybe" was only a fantasy, not a reality. Who can tell another man his thoughts?

Kenneth Hunt

In the Santa Lucia mountains several miles from the Big Sur coast, a friend of mine, O. Lloyd Hicks, was helping me chop firewood. We saw a fresh cougar track near the redwood cabin and heard the animal's piercing screams coming down the rugged canyon.

For over twenty years Hicks had been wandering throughout the West, stopping now and then to fix fence on some ranch, help out at a logging camp, or work at construction jobs. He looked up at the animal's sounds and said thoughtfully: "I'm a lot like that cougar up there. He's not hostile or vicious, but he doesn't like to be cornered. He likes to be left alone, to have his own way of living. Both the cougar and I can stand just so much of people and civilization. I'm a loner. I guess you could call me a Human Cougar."

This reawakened memories of my boyhood in Perris, California, where on a clear day in winter you could see snow-capped mountains in three directions: Mount Baldy, Old Greyback, and San Jacinto. That was in the early 1930s, before southern California was engulfed by the great migrations from the Dustbowl, the Depression, and World War II.

In my boyhood we used to go down to the San Jacinto River after it rained to catch rattlesnakes as they crawled out from the rocks along the riverbed in search of higher ground. Our teacher sold the venom, and the money was used to buy glass beakers and test tubes for the high school chemistry class. In this semiarid region, I remember how we planted barley, which never quite made threshing worthwhile, and milked the scrawny but dependable family goats; and I remember the apricot-drying shed, where you could meet people who were from other places, even Mexico.

High school was all right, but it was more exciting down along the railroad tracks, for I never knew for sure who might be there: someone with a different story, with a different way of looking at the world, and often a need I could fill in return. There was the little bakery that let me have a loaf of "day-old" bread for a nickel. Putting the loaf into the basket hooked on the handle bars, I'd bicycle down the dirt road along the tracks to the edges of town where I would almost always find one or more tramps, road kids, or drifters camped out in the weed patches and tamarisk trees that were commonly called "jungles."

To this day I remember asking a fellow there who was about my age, fifteen: "What do you want to be when you grow up?" I can still see his perplexed expression and recall his hesitation from not having really thought about the problem in serious terms. He finally replied: "So, today I eat, tomorrow I'll go out looking. I'm real handy. I think I can do a bit of anything." Now, some forty years later, I suspect that there was a young Human Cougar in the making whose life would travel a very different path from mine.

For him life might be a series of immediate experiences, without consideration of causes and effects and without much planning for the future. He would wander the remote regions and small towns of the West. Curiosity occasionally might lead him to explore the hearts of the cities, but the tensions and hostilities he sensed there would encourage defensiveness, and he would escape back into closer touch with the inland valleys and mountains or the unfrequented coast.

Likely as not, my friend of that day subsequently took all of the western states and most of the South as home, changing habitat and work with the seasons and his moods. As with his four-footed cougar counterpart, he would only do what was absolutely necessary for survival. He would enjoy his freedom and live in the present, both of which would become more difficult as laws and regulations, job requirements, and seniority rosters began to hem him in. Throughout all of this he probably was unwilling to knuckle under to regimentation, and as his own physical vitality waned, he would find the human and economic environments increasingly unacceptable and alien.

This young man was not a hobo or bum, hippie, beatnik, or Bohemian in the usual sense. It was his kind who developed the frontier, cleared the land and made it productive, worked the mines, turned forests into houses, and brought about the conveniences of modern life. Other than for the satisfaction of participating and doing, there were few carry-over rewards, at least not economic ones, for his kind roamed on toward the next horizon. Nature and solitude and the unknown were his framework.

If you are a Cougar and there are the open spaces, the road ahead, the railroad track, the stream, the highway, who is to resist what may be around the next bend?

Tonight or tomorrow in the café or tavern there may be that good woman who will have you, and you will want to have her and treat her as a woman should be treated: come home to her, protect her, love her. That she is so rarely found makes the quest all the more important. Whether you are looking for the eternal feminine, for attributes you dimly feel your mother had, or for the warmth and protection and possible excitement of the womb, one cannot be sure. It is certainly not the same as looking for the one-night stand, and it is not wanting a family and home to settle down with forever. It is somewhere in between, a vague concept that lasts just so long, only long enough to refresh you for the next experience.

No one quite seems to understand you, and you are not much help in explaining yourself. You quite possibly have never even thought about doing so. Yours is not a philosophy in the sense of having a carefully thought-out viewpoint. You just prefer giving to receiving, action to inaction, challenge to security. You accept being the logger rather than the paper manufacturer; the prospector, not the assayer; the cowhand, not the feed lot operator; the laborer, not the contractor.

You were seldom a member of any athletic team. You were never a "team player" and never quite understood team effort, even though you liked people. The good of the team over the individual was foreign to your way of thinking. Boxing and scrapping and outdoor activities that test the individual came naturally. Swimming, archery, fishing, hiking, and cycle-racing are all to your liking. You may have tried your hand in the rodeo.

In essence, this is the type of person who built the West. This is the individual without whom there would be no Seattle, Albuquerque, Barstow, or Dallas today. Now the nation's economy has changed. Society is suffocating from too many rules. There seems to be no place for the Cougar —that is, unless he makes major changes within himself, most of which would not square with his notions of individuality and free choice. Rarely protesting, picketing, or clamoring for government handouts, seldom voicing cries of injustice or hatred toward real or imagined oppressors, largely unaware of much tragedy in life, and free of self-recrimination, the Cougar accepts his life as his own eulogy.

My wife and I have become acquainted with many Cougars and individuals with Cougar strains during the past several decades. Our interest has not been sociological, psychological, or reformist. Rather, we have sought understanding of individuals who seem to embody so many fine traits. They have provided us with new perspectives on our own everyday philosophies and values and unconsciously given us new insights into our own personalities.

With no group identity or advocacy in his behalf the Cougar in our midst often roams about undetected. Some understanding of the historical period in which he was the pride of the land can help us identify and get to know this unobtrusive human species.

# They've Long Been Around

I like challenges in life. I like to do things I know
other people would give up. I know where I'm at,
where I'm coming from. There's this feeling for the
past. I've thought of life as a cowboy with a six-shooter
riding a horse. You can say you can take me out of the
West, but you can't take the West out of me.

Louis "Luke" Miller,
a Cougar in his thirties

Relentless changes have been altering our nation at an
incredible rate. Within the past fifty years, most of New

17

England's farms have reverted to woodlands, as have the cottonfields of the Gulf States. Monstrous machines have opened the earth's crust to get at the black gold of Appalachia and the Ohio River basin. Western prairie has become farmland, and hundreds of valleys and canyons are now man-made lakes. Older fruit orchards and market gardens have yielded to the sprawling subtopias. Hills have been severed by superhighways to accommodate trucks. We used to look at the sky for the source of a bird's song; now we look upward to determine what kind of plane is creating the thundering crescendo. But the changes in our symbolic world have been even more fundamental. The floods of words from radio, TV, and newspapers have given people the possibility of playing passive roles. Instead of experiencing directly, they can learn, work, and love entirely with and through words. Our natural environment is obscured by layers of verbalization.

To be sure, there is more pioneering in some regions than in others. Alaska is still a mecca for the hardy and adventurous. In Arizona the pioneering spirit is slackening, even though it qualified for statehood as recently as 1912.

Looking back just a little further—and not very much at that—the urban West has had a short history. In 1880 Leadville, Colorado, had a larger population than Los Angeles, California! A couple of decades before that, California's largest town, for a brief time, was Volcano, where today there are only 150 inhabitants tucked in the crater hollow.

We have finally realized, and to a certain extent accepted, that the countryside is changing, dying, and being reborn. We are being reconciled to the shifts and changes that have taken place in the family, even when we have not understood them. For many of us these changes have been confusing, startling, and painful. Glancing backward can help us be more sensitive to some of these shifts in class and social structure. Understanding where we came from can help us understand where we are and where we are headed. That knowledge can help us make our own decisions more wisely and help make those changes less wrenching if not more pleasant.

The opening of the American West came about through the determination of adventurers looking for pelts and gold and missionaries hell-bent upon changing the beliefs of the Indians. Accompanying and following in the footsteps of these pioneers were men and women willing to risk all to achieve a new life. For these people almost anything was better than sticking around trying to patch up an intolerable family situation, or being arrested on circumstantial evidence and unjustly convicted for a crime by misguided sheriffs, juries, and judges. If your old man was "hard-nosed," going West offered the chance to prove yourself to yourself and the rest of the world, too. Or maybe you wanted to get married, and in your neck of the woods the pickings were pretty slim.

Certainly, many a strong-headed girl, rather than marry the local evangelist or Bible belter, preferred to take her chances by launching off into the great unknown. And unknown it was. Even though she might be able to read, there were no books telling her what she might find beyond the Mississippi—no radio reports, no motion pictures, no TV, no photographs. Just a few secondhand tales from the visiting drummer. Many of these young women would be the envy of some modern-day liberationists. Equality was a foregone conclusion, since it took the combined efforts of all adults to make a go of the western trek.

Life out there was challenging, and a person had to

work at survival. Land had to be cleared and filled to make passable roads. Fields had to be leveled and cultivated. Livestock had to be acquired and tended. Lean-tos had to be replaced with houses. Ways of providing medical treatment had to be developed, and the young had to be given some formal education. Since people lived together in communities rules had to be made and enforced. The demands upon the ordinary adult were far different from the demands upon most of us today. Self-seeking humans and untamed nature made for daily dangers and uncertainties. Death was no stranger.

In the last century the nature of the land and our environment has helped to shape the people. The Deep South developed large-scale plantations and a biracial system. North of the Ohio and Missouri, the rugged winters made for spurts of intensive industriousness, and the land was level enough for clearing and planting. Then there was the hilly belt stretching from the Carolinas across West Virginia, Kentucky, Tennessee, Missouri, Arkansas, and into Oklahoma. The people who settled and stayed in these areas were, on the whole, independent and kept apart from the mainstream of the nation. The Kentuckian or Arkie had his own place in the scheme of things; he could grow some vegetables, juice up with white lightning, cut a little firewood for the winter months, and live with very little coming in or going out.

The vigor of the industrial revolution in northeastern America called for an increasing flow of basic commodities and foodstuffs. The momentum westward brought changes first to those areas most easily reached by streams and trails. The prairies beckoned, and the plains were penetrated by steel rails. Agriculture became possible on a large scale with rail cars going hundreds, even thousands, of miles. Hazardous cattle drives were replaced by quick, dependable transportation to the yards of the new towns of Chicago, Cincinnati, St. Louis, Memphis, Omaha, and Kansas City. The growth of these cities created an enormous demand for construction labor. Industries ringing the Great Lakes called for vast quantities of coal and timber and innumerable other natural resources. Hands were needed to harvest crops and maintain roadbeds for the trains. Machinery was scarce and unpredictable. Muscle was king!

The individual who could follow the harvest in the spring from Texas northward was in demand, and the hard worker enjoyed prestige. These working drifters were ever pushing on; they opened up Wyoming, Idaho, Oregon, and all of the West. As a class these fellows accepted uncertainty and believed in an honest day's work for a day's pay. Thousands of them roamed the American heartland, the Rockies, and the regions bordering the Great American Desert. Sometimes these men had families and would return home in the winter—home being almost anywhere. Wages were low, but a little savings could go a long way when carried back to a Kentucky hollow where wants were simpler than those of today.

In a sense these tramps were the pride of the nation. They filled useful functions and moved on when their tasks were done. Sometimes they would make a sufficient grubstake to homestead, or to return to some point and settle down as a local merchant, or go on to get more education and enter a profession. Some made their home base for part of each year in the workingmen's hotels on West Madison in Chicago, Larimer Street in Denver, Main Street in Los Angeles, or wherever there was an inexpensive hotel. The cities and towns were expanding; there was no talk of urban destruction or urban renewal.

But the whole working scene in America has been changing as machines have become more efficient and more prevalent. The thirty men who used to be needed in a mine tunnel have been replaced by a crew of three with a boring machine and a rock carrier. Even mucking (cleaning out a mine drift) has become largely automated. The Fresno scraper was pulled by mules. It was wonderful in its day, but that day is gone.

Agribusiness employs huge threshing machines. Tomatoes, lettuce, and other vegetables are now packed with the help of machines. "Factories in the field" is no longer just a phrase. And the fruit picker is finding himself in some instances competing with a mechanical tree shaker.

Helicopters and balloons are now used in logging operations. Fishing fleets have sonar and radar devices and mechanical hoists to sweep in catches.

Thus, no longer do we have an expanding economy largely based on a floating population of seasonal workers. Unionization has closed the workers into ranks and checkmated the vindictive boss and greedy owner. With increasing wages have come job stability and health benefits—that is, for those willing to stay in one place. Settling down brings with it the gratification and demands of stable family life—houses, furniture, automobilies, travel, and even pensions. These changes have come about through the workers yielding up a measure of their freedom and individuality, through toeing the line and abiding by the restrictive rules of those in government, business, and the unions who play their various institutional games.

Keeping up with the Joneses has become more than a catchphrase. People look around and size up what their neighbors have. By contrast the old-time tramp with his bindle—a couple of blankets, an extra shirt, and an extra pair of socks rolled in a piece of canvas—might have nothing against today's life-styles and possessions but merely value other things more highly. He would be happy to see his wife acquire possessions, yet as often as not he sees possessions as irrelevant to living and loving. More frequently than statistics can show, the marital nest built upon a common-law understanding falls apart under the tramp's own inadequacies as a provider, and invariably his own lack of interest in facing the challenge of contemporary life puts him to flight.

In our day a young man can hardly risk taking off to make his way as he works and grows. Unionization has fostered a static society. The restless individual finds he must not only have a union card or a civil-service classification but must be able and willing to stick around until an opening comes his way. And the strictures of seniority rosters can quickly dim eager desire. Other than in the declining opportunities to work the harvests, references are needed to get a job and where can a tramp get a work history in order to get work?

When the sawmill closes for a while or the mine temporarily suspends operations until new financing is arranged, increasing numbers of people must learn to live on welfare or aid to dependent children.

But not *all* the working tramps. There is one kind who doesn't wait around for the reopening of the mill, mining camp, or the upward swing in the economy. His roots are in the land, not the institutions. For him one place is not necessarily better than another. He glories in the experience of the day and knows that at times it is more satisfying to be sleeping under the stars than to be quilted down on box springs in four-walled comfort. He desires satisfaction from new challenges and new risks. He doesn't condemn the sedentary "home guard," those who like permanence; he doesn't even feel sorry for them. On the whole he feels that they must select their own life beat and live as they wish.

Sometimes the Cougar thinks of the days that were, days when the working tramp was respected and when the Cougar type had a sense of his own range and belonging thereto. But the conditions that made him master have changed, and now there is almost no territory left in which he can feel dominant.

# What Cougars Aren't

Hobo, tramp, bum, wino, fruit tramp, migrant farm laborer, hippie, beatnik, beachcomber, hard-road freak, street person, flower child, runaway, splitter, floater, road kid, Bohemian, nomad, and vagabond: these are some names commonly applied to those who have adopted drifting as a way of life. To these I would add "Cougar."

To understand this species I will summarize the types of drifters. This will make it easier to identify the Cougar.

Besides having a measure of rootlessness, most drifters have dropped out of the mainstream of conventional society. They haven't the drive and determination to earn the traditional status symbols or to accumulate possessions. They are less inclined than most people to aim for a goal, such as becoming a lawyer, boss, or head of nurses; they tend to live each day as it comes. They don't bemoan the fact that learning gained while sitting on a park bench doesn't lead to an academic degree. Drifters usually feel that their decision making and independence are more fundamental than planning for the future or any static security. While shunning or claiming to reject most traditional institutions, such as church, school, or the government, they may know next to nothing about them.

The percentage of younger to older drifters is increasing. This trend has to do with the relentlessly increasing power of government and unions. Under the name of urban renewal, the winter homes of the older working drifters in city centers have been destroyed and replaced by temporary parking lots awaiting the execution of new inner-city plans. When a species' habitat is destroyed, it doesn't necessarily adjust or move on. Sometimes it simply dies out more quickly than it might have otherwise.

Drifters under thirty sometimes speak of themselves as "freaks" and look for their status within a counterculture. As "outsiders" they are on tributaries of the mainstream of America. Paddling or floating along in their personal canoes, they often appear to be going nowhere in particular.

Throughout our land the rootless young are experimenting with new ways of living and achieving self-reliance. In rural America there is a resurgence of subsistence gardening and farming and experimentation with extended family and communal living.

In the cities one overhears fragments of conversations that echo nonconventional sentiments: "Make love, not hate." "You're an Aries, wow!" "She's a Libra and you know what you can expect. . . ." "Far out." "Got a joint? . . . a dubie?" "My old man told me. . . ." "Where can I crash?" "Who needs knowledge anyway? It took them three thousand years to mess things up. We've learned more in three months. . . ." "The universe is mine, it's me. . . ." "I'm the center of the divine light. . . ." "He is perfect peace and perfect truth. . . ." "We're all bisexual I think . . . ." "It's real. . . ." "Superconsciousness brings release. . . . OommmmPa. . . . OommmmMa. . . . Oommmm, it's good, it's good. . . ." "Right on. . . ."

In the last half-dozen years, people have tended to apply the term *hippie* to the many varieties of younger drifters. Within the counterculture the term has been losing currency, particularly since young people are increasingly recognizing differences among themselves.

Nevertheless, "hippie" is still part of our language, and I asked a thirty-four-year-old Cougar what he thought about the term. He scratched his head, thought for a moment, and said, "I can't really say what a hippie is. I guess the way society thinks of them is people who want to do their own thing the way they want to. I think they have a better understanding with each other and with the world than most people. Many hippies are wandering around with no destination. But with most of them it's probably a means of transportation rather than a way of life. Most of them go back home or to school or back to the cities. There aren't many like me."

Then I asked an older Cougar who has roamed western North America for some twenty years whom he would call a hippie and what differences he has noticed among drifters. When I saw him a week later in the kitchen of a cabin in the redwoods, he had a stack of poems alongside the kerosine lamp. These are the first poems he had ever written.

## THE HIPPIE

My hair is long, but that's righteous man.
My course in life is without a plan.
Right on, Right on.
Society says I'm a natural freak,
The way I dress and the way I speak.
Right on, Right on.
My life is mine to waste or gain.
Man, I'm not out for fortune or fame.
Right on, Right on.
Grass and pills are way out man.
When on the stuff, it's crazy land.
Right on, Right on.
Yeah, I'm a Hippie, I dig it dad.
It's the best damn life I ever had.
Right on, Right on, Right on.

Kenneth Hunt

In the 1920s some of the young viewed themselves as Bohemians or vagabonds. Sections of New York, Boston, Chicago, St. Louis, New Orleans, Hollywood, and San Francisco were given over to Bohemian living. At the same time there were those who roamed the nation as vagabonds or as working tramps.

## BOHEMIANS

In some ways we're nonconformist
doing our very own thing.

We project our innermost feelings

in art, in writing and dealing.

Our social life is weird I guess.
Simplicity seems to be our quest.

We create the unknown beauty,
The Mona Lisa, music to obscurity.

In Levis, sneakers and shirts hanging out
we dwell among our creations, 'cause
that's what it's all about.

Kenneth Hunt

In the economically unsettling years of the 1930s, hundreds of thousands of teenagers, often through necessity, left their homes in search of the basics of survival. They were road kids whose days varied from beachcombing to migrant farm labor. Today's nomads and vagabonds are much more likely to be on trips with an aspiring ecological, religious, or philosophical intent.

## THE NOMAD, 1974

I seek solitude for quiet meditation.
I wander the land without obligation.
Free to believe in what I choose.
Unlike Catholics, Christians or Jews.
I glory pain.
Off the vine and trees I eat.
Shedding clothes to capture sun's heat.
Nature's my God, my religious belief.
For her I suffer voluntary grief.

I glory pain.
I'm not sorry nor am I sad,
I'm just a wanderer called Nomad.

Kenneth Hunt

World War II took over the lives of most individuals during the 1940s. It was difficult not to be part of a work or military establishment.

In the 1950s the flowering of the beatniks was nurtured by Jack Kerouac, Lawrence Ferlinghetti, Russell Joyner, Neal Cassady, Allen Ginsberg, Ken Kesey, Eric Nord, and other intellectuals. They clustered in San Francisco, Venice, New Orleans, and New York, tending to be more literary and less arty than the Bohemians. Some aging beats are still around, especially in northern California, Oregon, and Boulder, Colorado.

The flower children, a phenomenon of the late 1960s, converged upon the Haight-Ashbury section of San Francisco. Across the bay in Berkeley, there was a commingling of students with political activists, hustlers, and the generally disenchanted.

In the early 1970s, both of these areas underwent change. Three significant categories of drifters to be found now in many major cities are the street people, the road people, and the hard road freaks.

At loose ends, the street people make out as best they can on the street. Sponging off the psychologically susceptible and those willing to share, they have developed many devices and techniques for obtaining the necessities of life. Many of them capitalize on their personalities by effective exhibitionism. As other impressionable young desert them, they look for ways of getting into the public economic trough or returning to traditional living.

## STREET PEOPLE

On a park bench or along the same street
You'll see us there, that's where we meet.

Sun up until dawn we patiently wait
for some real happening to guide our fate.

Some are here by choice alone
Others because of broken homes.

We're outsiders, the left-out kind.
No culture restraint, oblivious of time.

Living for the present, tomorrow for hope
Panhandling for food, perhaps for dope.

Work is a problem, unlike years before
it's real rough to live any more.

When conditions change, thereafter complete
Perhaps then, diminishing people of the street.

Kenneth Hunt

Road people, on the other hand, are usually more mature and self-sustaining. Often they work as trash haulers, at odd jobs, in restaurants, or at a craft. Unweighted by possessions, they travel about a great deal. Many have decorated vans or campers carefully fitted out for sleeping. These modern gypsies and vagabonds survive by virtue of our affluent society.

Hard road freaks are the skilled hustlers who exploit the weak and impressionable. Frequently they push drugs, and both males and females are likely to try their hand at pimping. Living by their wits, they are physically and verbally aggressive. Their very ruthlessness appeals to the admiring young from well-regulated homes. Embodying power and evil, some of these hard road freaks have achieved dominance over members of their own ethnic groups. Their mystique is similar to that enjoyed by some of the gurus and leaders of mystic cults.

## HARD ROAD FREAK

Don't be proud cause I'm certainly not
Man, I'm out to take what ever you got.

I might stop over for a day or week.
That's how I got the rep as a hard road freak.

Hustling, cheating and feloniously at work
relieving possessions of some poor jerk

I manipulate by sheer brute force
The young and innocent of course.

So I hit the asphalt for a couple weeks
that's why we're called the hard road freaks.

Kenneth Hunt

The classifications for middle-aged drifters might well be as follows: bum or hobo, migrant fruit picker, tramp, wino, and Cougar. Although people used to speak of the *working* hobo, today tramps look down upon hobos, who exist largely through bumming. Hobos or bums generally live in cities and receive handouts from individuals or from governmental and social-service agencies. They have no desire or intention to work in exchange for benefits received.

"You've been roaming the West for many years. How could you compare the older and the younger drifters?" I asked John Atkinson, a reflective Cougar in his middle thirties. Atkinson said: "Among nonworking drifters, most bums, I believe, don't work if work can be avoided and are without a decent amount of compassion for the wants and needs of others. They do what's required to obtain money for wine, to escape reality for as long as possible. The "road kids" as I see them, aren't really aware of what they want from life. They unhesitatingly strive for free handouts to avoid employment and often try to become a part of the welfare system."

Bums even mooch from tramps, and many a jungle on the outskirts of a western town where the tramps bed down for the night is likely to be visited by a bum or two. They stand around watching the mulligan cook and sooner or later may be invited to have some.

Most bums get all of the welfare they can, discovering that that is the way to fit into society's framework.

## THE HOBO

I lost my guts some time ago.
What happened to me I do not know.
I bum the streets and I bum the bar.
It seems I've bummed forever near and far.

I bum for drinks and I bum for bread.
I'm not a strong man, in fact I'm easily led.
I won't work for a measly crumb.
I get by just being a bum.

                              Kenneth Hunt

Al Lawless, an old-time hobo with many Cougar characteristics, gave this thumbnail analysis as he waited for a
passing freight: "If you're a rough man you can take it. It's
a hard living, but it shows what you can accomplish without
money or power. I guess it's sort of like the frontier life of
years ago." He went on to explain. "Very few young people
are riding trains, and the old hobos are finding it harder.
Trains move faster now and getting on is harder. Besides,
welfare is encouraging everyone to stay put. . . . About fifteen years ago I settled down in Montana long enough to
hold a steady job and get good clothes and a car. But the
problem in Billings was that every time I heard a train
whistle I had to fight myself from going back on the tracks.
And one night I went down there and just rode out of town.
It was the freest damn feeling in the world. I haven't settled
down since."

The modern tramp works intermittently and is there-
fore a part of the working class. However, he and the Al
Lawlesses are suffering from the growing inflexibility of our
changing institutions.

## TRAMP

My life is full of sadness, grief, and despair.
Even when I travel I seem to go nowhere.

I think of other people who do this very thing.
Who always seem to prosper yet never lose nor gain.
My life is very simple, without any certain goal.
I wander about a lonesome man, who's trying to find
    his soul.

Kenneth Hunt

If you are an older working tramp or drifter, you are likely to know some winos, all of whom seem to you to be somewhat inferior individuals. You know the bums drink wine. The smart-ass kids drink wine. The rich drink wine. The labor contractors bring in wine to keep you stupefied and make a profit. At one time or another almost all drifters drink wine.

There is only one time a tramp or drifter is willing to go the wine route thoroughly. That is when he has decided that his days are numbered and he is prepared to give up. Then he joins the Frisco circle and pitches in his dime or quarter and drinks and drinks and drinks. Two years, three years, four years: it won't last long. The drifter knows this, but he chooses this life only after he feels he is getting old, say forty-five or fifty. The transition from drifter to wino is a transition from life to death. Once started, the drifter holes up in skid row, ceases experiencing, and starts listening for his own "taps."

The drifter knows he is no longer the man he was, and he hastens his self-destruction. The brotherhood of the wino can achieve an almost mystical level and generates a contempt for the bum who is not a wino. Some tramps, finding themselves entering this period of psychological decay, expose themselves to tremendous risks, and it is hard to say whether their end comes by suicide or by accident.

## THE WINO

I drink to get drunk.
I drink not to think.
I drink not to live.
I drink to oblivion.

Kenneth Hunt

Among the roamers and drifters, the Cougar stands out as a distinct type. His characteristics and attributes definitely set him apart. He has been overlooked primarily because of his independence and self-containment. Now that we have seen what he is not, we owe it to the Cougar and to ourselves to learn more about this neglected human species.

# Five Cougars
# Speak for Themselves

ERIC FURBISH

"Caballo Blanco" (White Stallion) is what his fellow field-
workers call Eric. Tall, lanky, and blond, with a ruggedly
handsome face, he looks like a Viking god. He has tried his
hand for more than thirty years at mining, logging, fishing,
fruit and vegetable work—a self-styled jack-of-all-trades
with a tendency towards quiet contemplation and a great
love of beauty.

"I worked in the Lucky Friday mine up in Idaho in
sixty-three. It was a good mine but the ground was sick—
water seepage, seams, making the ground loose. Like an

overripe watermelon would crack, that's the way the ground would crack. And there were air blasts all the time. Nobody knows where they come from. Those scientists try to figure them out, but nobody knows. Sometimes they'd hit you like a big freight train loaded with nitroglycerin.

"The tunnels were held up with rock bolts: six-foot steel rods—drill a hole, put one in, put a board on it, and then a steel plate and then cinch it up. On the other end *don't* of the rock bolt is an expanding piece of steel— *have to* that's what you tighten up. If you tighten it too *rock-* much it snaps. Periodically when you come on the *bolt* shift (I was on the third shift), you take a double *the sky* jack and hit the ones you put in. If they thump, it's OK. If they ring a little, there's weight on them. If they ring like a church bell, there's too much weight and you have to put another one in. You can also tell if that plate is embedded into the wood too deep and it's carrying too much weight.

"Back at AS&R in 1947 they used to use timbering. The newer thing is not much safer. Sometimes used to get cheap steel from Japan. You'd set it up and screw it in and it would snap. I got off at 7:00 a.m. I'd have such a knot in my stomach every day, I'd go and drink beer and it'd take me hours to get it unwound—from the tension and strain of being down there. Used to say, gonna get me a job on the outside for a dollar an hour—don't have to rock-bolt the sky.

"There was high-grade ore in that mine. One time we were in a tunnel drilling. A six to eight foot vein. Pure silver. Guys would put it in their pockets, bring it out, give it to friends.

"And then we started hearing these cracks—like a house cracking, like the sharp crack of a rifle—from out in the big room. I know there was too much ground open—it was about twenty-five by thirty feet. Too much ground open. If it ever comes in you're sealed like a rat. So we heard this loud crack. My partner Duffy says what we gonna do? I say stand right here. He wanted to run. He would have run right out into the cave-in—I had to hold him by the shirt. There's usually a second crack following the first one, but we waited and it didn't come. Got to thinking about that big crack all over that room. The sound of it seemed like it went to the very ends of all the rock bolts and seamed the whole ceiling. My idea was to put in six-foot and also eight-foot rock bolts to hold the seam together—would stop the slubbing.

"You could only work five or six hours a day under-ground. That was enough. We used to get five cents a run-ning foot for everything you drill—also five cents a running foot for everything you'd slush out.

"A glory hole is when there's a blow back. The first stick you put in has to be tightened so it will explode. Then you set six to seven sticks of powder in the same hole. If powder isn't tamped it'll blow and the rest of the powder won't blow. That makes the ground sick for the next drill. Sometimes the ground wouldn't even hold the weight of the stinger, and the only way I could drive would be to get a foothold and hold the thing in my arms. That's a lot of pressure against your arms.

"There's a place called the keyboard, which is like a gate, like crawling through a barbed wire fence. Some guys instead of going down into safety would just stand *hang* by the keyboard for the blasts. There's no safety *fire!* standing there. The boards could break and cave down. You could get concussion of the eardrums. They were Finlanders—not crazy, just didn't want to go down—it was a waste of time. I always used to go way down. Then you'd sit and count the blasts. Say there were thirty holes, you'd count the counts. Sometimes they'd go off together so fast you couldn't keep track. So you count up, and if you and your partner only got twenty-nine, you know there's a hang fire—one didn't go off. So then you use water or you write "hang fire" on a piece of cardboard and hang it up there so the next shift knows. If you drill there it goes off and blows you clean across and tacks you against the wall and there you are.

"There's a sickness of nerves down there—a fear, a tightness. Those airblasts—no one knows where they come from. Boom. Boom. And rocks come slubbing down all the time. You gotta keep your head down. Without that helmet my head would have been smashed like an egg. One time I was working as a timberman's helper. They were pushing a 400-foot raise. We were about 200 or 275 feet up, repairing the muck-shoot where the waste goes down. The boards get broken from the stuff falling down, so we were putting up new boards. They drill at a 56-degree angle. We were working on an angle on the skip. You gotta hang on to everything.

"Everything was going fine, and then we heard this boom boom boom. What's that? Sounds like a big chunk of mud coming down. We had it all planned before, *boom* where who would go for safety so we wouldn't be *boom* bumping elbows. He snugged up against one side. *boom* My place was to hide behind the skip. I had to hang on with a fist grip and didn't have time to lower my head far enough. That thing came crashing down and knocked my hat clear off and all I seen was rainbow colors, but I kept my grip somehow.

"I lost my eye, dislocated my shoulder, lost the use of

my knee. I was two weeks in the hospital. After the accident, they put me back in the same place to test if my nerves would get stronger or weaker. I got pretty cold and sweaty. I thought everything was coming down on me all the time. Things just didn't go right after that. I worked for two more weeks and then quit. Boss said what are you quitting for? If I go back in there I might endanger others' lives and my own.

"Lucky Friday was a good mine, but bad ground. Lots of sugarquartz—like trying to drill a hole in a sugar bowl."

•          •          •

## FROM EARLIER DAYS, CA. 1939

"The company that bought the sawmill out put their own men in our places and we hadda go. So, one of the fellers says let's go on up to Oregon, work in the hopfields. That's all right with me.

"And so, we proceeded on up to Salem. We bought food and we bought gas, and it wasn't long before the little money I had ran out and the money they had had
*gettin'* run out, so we proceeded to bum gasoline as we
*by* went along the line. I had a Coleman stove, a three-burner Coleman stove. Every time we'd stop and want some gas we'd take that stove with us, and they'd give us the two gallons of gas and let us keep the stove, and then we'd run that two gallons out and the car would stop and we'd wait for somebody to come by, oh, a tractor or something, and ask him if we could get a couple gallons of gas for this here stove.

"Well, we done it pretty good, until we got halfway and you know then one of the guys we was going to trade the stove with for gas, he did take the stove, and we got the two gallons of gas and that was the end of having the stove. From then on we had to mooch with nothing.

"It was my turn to ask for some food. This was real new to me. I went up to the farmhouse and asked. Who appeared in the door but a young girl my age. Real pretty. Well, I sure stammered and got all lumped up. Boy, I couldn't speak, so I just asked her could you tell me what time it is, and I left.

"But we made it all the way up. We got to Oregon, to Salem. And we started looking around the hopfields. Well, *never did make $2.00* we got a job in the hopfields all right. We went to pickin' that day and I made 30 cents off pickin' the hops. We all had an idea that we'd all go real early before the sun got up and pick till the sun went down, then we might have a little bit of money. We did do that. I never did make $2.00! $1.50 or $1.60, something like that. Never went to town with $2.00 in my pocket.

"So at the end of that hops—we stayed in a little old kind of like a smoke shed this feller had—he came over to us one day, me and old Chuck Goddard, and wanted to know if we would cut some cordwood for him. Sure. Well, he said he'd give us $1.60 for sixteen-inch stuff and $1.25 for four-foot stuff.

"So we done it. We got a cord up. We never could get two cords a day, cause we had some tools that were unbelievable—more like antiques. And with that, I never did get to town with $2.00 in my pocket. We'd get a cord up and go down and see him and get our money. It'd be $1.25 or $1.60—we never did make $2.00. But we could sure get a lot of stuff with the $1.60 or $1.25. Everything was a dime and a nickel."

"I don't like to be crowded for time. You always button your shirt wrong hurrying, or leave your fly open or something. You worry about etiquette, you spill the *I like* gravy. I've traveled in freight cars, boxcars, first-*to* class airplanes. I like to travel alone. You can go *travel* where and when you want to go—you don't have to *alone* wait on anybody. When you're with somebody, you've got to put yourself all the way in them or not at all. You have to make sacrifices."

MELVIN L. SETTLE
Mel was a self-supporting logger in the Sierra Nevada by age thirteen. Since then he has worked the mines, ranches, and fields of theWest. His face is deeply lined by years of experience—years he has enjoyed.

●        ●        ●

"Most of the time I worked on ranches I was loading, bucking hay, loading boxes, or swamping sacks of barley, wheat, and potatoes, although I drove truck some and have worked in potato sheds, cotton gins, and packing houses.
"Really the most interesting thing is not the experiences you have in the fruit but that if you follow it you see a lot of country and are always meeting new people. That is *living* what I like best about it for you can meet funny *from* ones good and bad ones every kind. You would be *day* surprised at what you can meet on the road if you *to day* try to. The best part to me I believe is that you have no responsibility or worries. You live from day to day and week to week never worrying about tomorrow—at least I never did."

## EUGENE MIHAILOVICH
With reddish hair, a gentlemanly manner and western-style clothes, he could be the tall and leathery-lean man in the Marlboro ad. He has made western America his odyssey, working at occupations as varied as stunt man and house painter.

•          •          •

"The snow started falling, and all the kids in town were very happy because they knew that their families would buy them new sleds, so they could play in the snow. My father bought me a big bobsled. And my brother and our friend next door and I slid down the hill to the slaughterhouse.

"It was about three months later when the siren at the coal mines blew and everyone knew that an accident had happened. We all waited for the news of what *accident* had happened, and pretty soon my friend's *at the* dad came and told my mom that our dad got his *coal* leg cut off just below the knee by an ore car. The *mine* car's brake didn't hold right and started going backwards and gaining speed as it came down the grade. My dad was the first one to see it and hollered a warning to the other miners to get out of the way, which they did. My father was on the opposite side of the track and when he ran he tripped on the rail as he was trying to get out of the car's way. But as luck would have it, it ran over his right leg, cutting it to the bone, which later had to be amputated. He was in the hospital for two weeks until his stump healed up and was brought home. The hospital furnished him with a pair of crutches until his wooden leg arrived, which my mom ordered through a mail catalog.

"Soon the leg arrived and my fears took hold of me.

There was something about that leg that scared the hell out of me. That was the first wooden leg I ever saw. It *chased* was ugly looking with a lot of holes and straps on *with the* it. I think my dad knew that it scared me, and to *wooden* make matters worse he would tell me that it was *leg* alive and would eat me up if I wasn't a good boy and, darn it, he would chase me around the room with it until my mom told him to knock it off and that I was only five years old and that it might do me some harm in my later years. So my dad said he was sorry and that he wouldn't scare me anymore. Boy, I was sure glad of that (whew).

"Soon my dad was walking as good as ever on his (shudder) wooden leg. It was just a few months later when my dad complained about the pain in his leg. My mom got worried over it, but my dad just laughed and said it wasn't anything to get upset about. Probably growing pains. I guess he said that to keep mom from worrying too much. Well it was forgotten until a few weeks later when he took off his wooden leg and saw the bluish pus and matter that came out of it. Mom rushed him to the hospital and the doctor told her it was cancer and that he would have to have it amputated above the knee or else it would get worse and he would die. So it was amputated. But with all the doctoring and pain remedies that was bought, the leg got worse and the pain unbearable.

"That same night when everyone was asleep, my dad went to the hotel just above where the boxing contest was held, registered there and then went to a liquor *that was* store and bought a fifth of whiskey. He then went *my dad* across the street and bought a bottle of strych- *a real* nine which he told the druggist he wanted to *man* kill some rats. He got it and went back to the hotel and drank the whiskey and chased it with the strychnine. They found him the next morning dead lying on the floor with a smile on his face. That was my dad. Not even afraid of death. He could drink with the best of them. Many times he drank them under the table. He was a real man and never took a back seat from any man.

"The whole town was really worried about it and tried to cheer my mom up as best they could. But it was quite a blow to her. She didn't know what to do with two little kids and no money left after paying for the wooden leg and dad's funeral expenses. Some of the town folks got up a collection for my mom to help with food and things. It's a good thing the house was bought and paid for. With no rent to worry about things were going smoothly for a while.

"Mom decided to go to work in the hospital and become a nurse. She left us with our grandparents to look after us until mom got off of work. At night mom would take some home courses in nursing, and after a period of time she became a full nurse on the hospital staff, an R.N. Mom paid all the folks that helped her back in full."

KENNETH HUNT
A droopy mustache and intense brown eyes dominate Kenneth's darkly brooding face. Well built and handsome, he looks a perfect typecast for any western movie. His highly developed powers of perception and a natural ability with words show in his poetry, which he started to write in his forties.

●          ●          ●

"My first job as a tramp had been in Yuma working in temperatures of 110 to 115 degrees on desert land as a cotton chopper or long-handle hoe operator. What it *out* means is that a cotton contractor would pick up *from* all the men as he could carry on the back of his *Yuma* pickup truck without dragging anyone from the back of it, which I had no doubt he would do if he thought he could get away with it. He could pile as many as forty men in an area of about a twenty-man capacity and would travel that way on given days anywhere from fifty to seventy-five miles daily, leaving town about 3:00 a.m. You had men sitting on your lap, hands, feet, and any place that was even partially available. You were very lucky if you got to the field without having had a broken bone somewhere in your body. All this for a buck and a half per hour. He would charge you a buck for the beautiful, pleasurable ride. (Punk!)

"What a racket! The field boss would carry with his crew in a separate car sandwiches, beer, wine, and soda pop. Everything cost $.50 with exception of wine. One fifth would cost you $2.25. A pint $1.25. The stores in town only charge $1.20 a fifth and $.60 a pint. You would have to work four hours before he would let you have any credit. And to top everything off, the boss didn't mind letting the workers know that if any of them brought their own wine or beer they would be fired and would have to make it back to Yuma the best they could. Seventy-five miles? It speaks for itself; all tramps were clean of booze.

"Not all the workers were tramps. Some were confirmed winos and would only work long enough to get their daily supply of juice (wine) and in all probability would be totally disabled before 2:00 p.m., passed out somewhere, snoring, defecating in his pants, some only urinating, some both, all exposed to the hottest time of day where it would be as high as 120 degrees.

"Some of the winos who weren't quite drunk but on the borderline would pile into the truck, and at least one or two would have what is known as the wino defecation (only it's a four-letter word). Drinking an excess of wine causes an overpowering bowel movement. It wasn't very pleasant riding back to town.

"In the early morn it is not so bad to work. It's fairly cool then. But around 11:00 it begins to get hot, and the hours ahead are most unthinkable. The sun is so intense that when I sweat it was like boiling water between my shirt and body. My back would be raw and sensitive and itchy like a thousand needle pricks. My eyes were red like two balls of fire from the glare of the sun's rays. Muscles became stiff and painful; I would get sick to the stomach and very sluggish by the end of the day.

"Many of the days in the field I had prayed silently for a different life. I prayed that this was all a very bad dream and that when I woke up I would find all the small comforts of home, under shady trees and all the wonderful things to go with it. But, day after day, I would punish myself solely to exist."

•          •          •

"Having a little pride left and a certain amount of feeling for my fellow man, I would never accept a free bed when I had money. Had I done this, I would only deprive some tired man out of a good night's sleep.

"So, having money and pride, I chose the Capital Hotel as a place to stay while I worked. This hotel was located on the mall on Main Street, but it was nothing more than a flop pad (room with a bed). It did have private rooms and not-too-clean bathrooms. I had to furnish my own towels, washrag, and soap. My room plus bath privilege cost a buck and a half per night so this was to be my home for the next two months.

"Oh! There was one more privilege furnished by the hotel and that was a TV set which was, and probably still is,

*TV brawls on and off screen* located in the main corridor for all to watch if so desired. TV was and still is my favorite escapism or pastime or whatever. I really dig the programs. But it had its problems too, because between winos, hobos, and tramps, each one half drunk or beyond, who were trying to outyell the other in trying to explain some past troubles of his to his

listener, . . . consequently the TV had to be turned up to the extent that it was impossible to concentrate on the picture tube, and as a result of the TV blasting away, the men in their rooms who had been trying to sleep would soon make a scene and they too would begin to shout and raise hell, "Knock that God damn noise off, you lousy bunch of sons!" Others yelling, "Turn that dirty fucking TV off!" "Break the SOB." "Throw a bottle at it! . . ." On and on it went until twelve midnight. I also done my share of yelling, like "Turn it up, sit down you crazy bastard, I can't see the picture." Some nights this action would end up in a brawl or more like a riot.

"One night I had just finished off my last can of a six-pack of beer between *Gunsmoke* and *Mission Impossible*. I might add that I was feeling pretty damn good, when this fellow about my age, weight and height, came marching chest out, fist doubled, clad only in his well-worn shorts, slamming his room door shut, he walked bravely, or stupidly, up to the TV and turned it off right in the middle of the *Elliot Ness FBI Story*.

"Now, anybody in his right mind would not dare do

such a lousy thing as that. So, me, thinking I was just as brave, or just as stupid, marched up and turn the TV back on. I shook my finger in his face and advised him not to do that any more. He must not hear so good because he ups and turns it off, I turn it on, he turns it off. We keep this routine going for what seemed to me a long time until I got mad and hit him in the kisser and he went down.

"I turned the TV on. When he got up, he landed a good one, just behind my ear, I went down, he turned the TV off. Nobody paid us any attention; most were preoccupied in their own little way. Anyway, we kept hitting, turning the TV, hitting, and turning until the manager who was quite drunk and who was also a fag, queer or queen, whatever, came out to inform everybody that it was midnight and time to turn the TV off (house rules) and that you 'sweet boys' should get some sleep. Boys?

"Anyway, it was this guy's turn to knock me down. Instead a big smile spread across his ugly puss. He had won. I felt cheated. He went to his room, redressed, came out, and grabbed my arm, and we marched like real troopers to the nearest bar to settle our differences over a few bottles of beer. This fellow was to become my best friend and traveling partner for some time until he slipped under the wheels of a boxcar when running to catch a freight."

LOUIS "LUKE" MILLER
A refugee from New Jersey, Luke is in his early thirties and has been on the road much of his life, often repairing roofs and painting houses. Slight of build, bearded, with intense expressive brown eyes, he looks at first glance like a "hippie," until you observe more closely.

•          •          •

"I like getting to know people. I watch people, how they act and what they do. Often when I just see someone sitting or standing, I say 'hi' and soon we're *a*   talking. Just friendly talk, without trying to gain *bunch*   something or beat them at something. Oldsters *of knots* usually enjoy talking to a stranger. And other *inside*   people do too. They can talk freely. Not like talking to their families or people they've got close relationships. So many people seem to have a kind of bunch of knots inside, and they have a need to talk and talking freely their shells crack. It makes me feel I'm doing something worthwhile, makes me feel real good."

# Early Life and Escape

When I was just a kid I always looked to my mom for food and love and my dad for learning and adventure.
                                                            Kenneth Hunt

In my youth in New Jersey when you were around eighteen to twenty you were supposed to look for a mate, get married, get a job eight-to-five, certain times for certain things. Anything else was not right. So I left.

I've always wanted to be on my own and do my own thing. It's made for a tougher life, but has freed me to do what I wanted to do, if I wanted to do it. And even in grade school I knew that the great big world out there belongs to everybody.

Louis "Luke" Miller

Although Cougars come from homes of almost any economic or social status, they are most likely to be from families in which one or both of the parents exhibited strong Cougar characteristics.

Most of my contacts with Cougars have been in the Far West, the Rockies, and the Midwest. Those I've met in or around Cougar crossroads—Vincennes, Louisville, St. Louis, Memphis, Pittsburgh, Butte, Cheyenne, Leadville, Denver, Waco, and Dallas—have told essentially the same stories about their upbringing and experiences as have those in other waystations like Walla Walla, Portland, Eureka, Oroville, Salinas, Stockton, and Los Angeles.

A great many speak of their Indian ancestry, the Cherokees being most frequently mentioned. They take pride in this ancestry and upon occasion refer to themselves as Indian, though they are often vague as to just which ancestor was what part Indian. This racial feeling seems to have had a strong influence on their attitudes since childhood. They seem to share a kind of romanticized range of stereotypes, both of the Indian and of the West of the last century. On the whole, Cougars come from white western European backgrounds, although I have known black, Oriental, Mexican, and Indian Cougars.

Most Cougars look back upon childhood as a happy time. They remember their childhoods with pleasure and generally seem to have been physically well coordinated and mature at an early age.

Eugene Mihailovich, in response to a letter, wrote of

his boyhood: "I was born in 1926 in a big red house on a hill
above a slaughterhouse shed in Roundup, Mon-
*the*       tana. It is a small town. The people there go out
*battle*    of their way to be nice and help others' families
*at*        in their needs and wants. When I was five years
*Roundup*   old, I was put in the ring to fight a big bully that
lived next door to us. The reason this incident
took place was because he always picked on my three-year-
old brother Richard. It got so bad that my brother couldn't
even go outside and play in the yard, unless the bully came
out and started trouble with him.

"Well, my dad got pretty fed up about the matter and
talked to the bully's dad about it. Oh, by the way, the bully
was a year older than I was. Well, my dad made a bet that I
could whip his son in a fair fight, and the bully's dad took
my dad up on it.

"It was a Saturday morning, and being a small town
the word got around that there was going to be a fight contest between the boy next door and myself. The bets started
mounting up pretty fast. The contest was to start at twelve
noon in the Roundup Tavern. People came from as far away
as Harlowtown, about sixty miles away, to see the contest.
The adults that were there first put up a ring in the center of
the tavern floor and two milking stools that some dairy
rancher donated for the contest.

"It was about eleven-thirty by then, and we got ready
to go to the tavern. We arrived at five minutes to twelve. My
dad took off my shirt, and I was left with my short-legged
pants and shoes. After a while the boy that I was supposed
to fight showed up with his dad, and they went through the
same procedure. A coin was tossed to see who would get the
right-side stool and vice-versa. Well, I won because my dad
called heads and it came up heads.

"The bartender had a cowbell hung up behind his bar to ring in case one of his customers buys the house a round of drinks. The bartender was voted as time keeper for the contest. My dad was my second and vice versa.

"There was some loud shouting about let the fight begin. Pretty soon the bartender rang the bell. I came out as the bell rang and circled my opponent looking for an opening to land a punch. But the other boy got the first one in and he hit me in the left shoulder. It hurt and I realized that he carried a good punch. Well, I figured it was my turn now, so I started jabbing with my left. I got him off balance and kept him that way and was always leery of his right fist. I finally saw an opening and landed a hard blow to the side of his head. He staggered back from the punch. His dad wanted to stop the fight on seeing his son's face and the red mark that was there, but the crowd booed him down and his dad let him stay in the ring. Oh, by the way, we didn't use boxing gloves. It was strictly bare knuckles.

"The second round was coming up. My dad gave me a talking to and told me if I didn't win that he would give me a licking when I got home. My dad was a big man, and he hit hard. No man in town would fight him. He was a coal miner, and he was strong.

"The bell sounded, I came out bound and determined to end the fight. I hit him with a left jab under the heart and followed with a hard right under the chin and knocked him over the ropes to win the contest. I know if I hadn't of won that I would be mighty sorry when I got home.

"The bartender held the stakes, and the money was given to my dad for me which he put in his big stetson hat. I got a lot of thanks and congratulations. They said that was the best fight they ever saw. After we left, the bartender sold drinks to the crowd. No drinks were sold to anyone during the fight. For a long time I was the talk of the town. And soon the bully and I became good friends and he never picked on my little brother again."

From the day he entered the classroom, the whole formal educational system was alien to the Cougar. "I didn't like the teacher up there telling me what to do" is the way one eighth-grade dropout explains his attitude toward school. This need not be surprising.

The traditional educational system has been refined to meet statistical averages of human learning and response. It has become geared to producing individuals who can pass certain kinds of tests at certain ages. Verbal skill and memory are most important. Looking alert, being cooperative, aiming to please the teacher, volunteering an answer whether you've thought it through or not, doing your homework, being on time, and above all else, having the knack and desire to get good grades are all interwoven into the educational fabric. The Cougar didn't fall in with this general program. As a youngster the Cougar was more likely to keep quiet if he felt he didn't understand something rather than to try to bluff through. Symbolizing and symbolic skills just weren't his strengths. Taking the word and orders of the teacher went against his grain.

Cougars are given to hand-mind performance; they had little inclination in school to make abstract interpretations and correlations. At recess time they would be eager to get out onto the playground and speed around. Body language and nonverbal communication were meaningful. Their interest in activity-oriented skills showed in their interest in practical matters, such as caring for plants and trees, preparing food, cleaning up trash, fixing cars, building structures, and caring for pets. Fixing something where there could be immediate visible improvement made sense to them.

Even more significant is the conflict between the idea and the immediate. For them, historical events, mathematical formulas, and generalizations of any kind held little meaning. An intellectual Cougar, Jon Bisinski (Jon the Vagabond), wrote: "As a 'politician' Bertrand Russell is simply an old fool. He knows a lot about Plato, but if he learned more about Plato he would know that mathematicians are simpletons. Mathematicians are good only when they have sure, certain premises. Then they can solve problems. The very fact that Russell wants to use mathematics to 'solve' philosophical or ethical problems is enough proof that his brain, or part of it, is very soft indeed. . . . I am so happy if I find people who do not agree with me and can explain it to me why they do not agree. Then and only then I learn much."

For young Cougars, formal education seemed worlds apart from day-to-day living. The world of books was different from what came across in conversations, over the radio, and from TV and theater screens. Cougars felt that the gap was too great to be bridged, or at least they lacked the desire to try to do so.

In addition, interest in girls often interfered with concentration in school. Although the young male Cougar didn't do very well in his studies, he found it possible to be happy with girls. Beginning at an early age with casual dates, he soon became involved with a particular girl. He might move in and then run away with her, possibly at a startlingly young age. The girl would usually be about his own age, but often somewhat more mature.

The whole setup seemed to provide a kind of congenial

atmosphere—at least in comparison with the classroom. However, when the girl wanted to stabilize and formalize the relationship, the young Cougar was unprepared educationally, economically, and psychologically. This was the time when the first underage drinking was likely to occur.

In prosperous homes individuals with Cougar tendencies are shielded from repetitive routines of education and living by those things money can provide: permissive schools, adventurous outdoor summer camps, years out to live on ranches or to travel, or employment in businesses owned by the family or friends. Some are brought back into the educational system after rebellious teenage years and eventually are worked into ranching, engineering, and other lines of work that permit variety of activity and relative freedom from regulation and human contact. Rarely will you find Cougars in law, accounting, in the church, or teaching, for in these fields it is important to put words and other symbols together, match sets of words, and be influenced and influence others by these.

Eric Hoffer, with his sixth-grade education, Bertrand Russell who never received a Ph.D., and the Cougar who left home and school in the ninth grade to explore the world around him have much in common. They learned in their own ways, and many of them surely merit Ph.D.'s in practical psychology and lifesmanship. As one of them told me, "I guess I'm a Roads scholar."

The Cougar may wish he had had more formal schooling, but not for a moment does he feel that the person who received more formal training is a better or wiser person than he. He recognizes the plain fact that education sometimes makes some things easier, such as acquiring money without real work and getting medical treatment if necessary.

In looking back over his younger years, the adult Cougar is likely to make remarks such as: "My dad was my idol—he was a settled man," or "They were always telling me what to do. I couldn't do it on that basis. Here's the thing. If I thought it could benefit, yes, I'd go along, because I wanted to. But not because I had to."

At best we can only generalize about the early life and education of Cougars, although there are strikingly similar attributes and patterns. In their early teens, Cougars were usually well liked and admired by classmates but tended to be restless to be doing actual things: to be earning money, traveling, or living with some girl. Their inclinations were in accord with the much-touted programs of today's experimental schools: learn by doing and experiencing. Take a project and carry it through. Avoid being taken in by symbols and labels. Do, know, and understand, allowing for more than rote memory and repetition.

Where there isn't much money in the family or where the parents aren't forward looking, they let the young Cougar escape. As he goes on in life, he tends to look back with real love and appreciation for his mother and usually respect and admiration for his father—this in spite of the fact that few Cougars were living with their parents after the age of seventeen.

Because of this, the families, parents, and young people alike, were spared the great traumas and disenchantment and tension experienced in most families when an eighteen- to twenty-five-year-old refuses to cooperate with the "grand plan." The parents submit to a kind of blackmail so that the young adult won't leave home and presumably get into trouble. Almost without exception the Cougar as a teenager did not follow his father's, stepfather's or mother's lover's advice, or for that matter any other adult male's.

The Cougar achieves his freedom just in the nick of time, perhaps sometimes a little too early. But it permits him a strong sense of self-identification and self-containment. He makes whatever he makes on his own, and his feelings are his, not those of the merchants or the fashion-mongers, the institutionalized social cliques or his family. He is never ashamed to say what he likes. If he likes the country music of Merle Haggard and Jerry Reed, he says so. If he hates acid rock, he doesn't pretend otherwise. If the poems of Edgar Guest are to his liking and he regards Jack London and *True* magazine as literature, he does not hesitate to say so. Without the encrustation of institutions, his entire being is exposed to the environment. Thus, he is less vulnerable to inner stresses but more vulnerable to ostracism by the man-on-the-street.

# Work Habits and Experience

You know I have a good job—I'm my own boss. That's a great deal of fringes to me. I can do what I want to do, take the time off when I want to take time off. I can sit down, get up, I can lay down, I can fall down, or I can work. I can do what I want to do. That's one of the greatest fringes in life, as far as I want in work. Nobody cracking the whip. Don't like that. Don't like to be pushed, don't like to be hurried. I like to take my time. I don't mind waiting for people. I don't like people waiting for me.

Eric Furbish

Actually, America's chief boon to the workingman is
that in this country the workingman can feel himself a
human being first. I doubt whether while thinking or
writing I am particularly aware of being a longshore-
man.

Eric Hoffer

You've gotta handle wood like you do people. Lift it up
and you know how it responds.

Frank Hoffman

Today you will find the Cougar mainly in the fields, on
ranches, or farming, still like their forebrothers
working the earth which is part of their very being. He
is a "doing" man who is constantly seeking out the
earth that needs him for his specialties, using farm
equipment, hand tools, chopping cotton with a short-
handle hoe, fruit picking, mining, felling timber in the
forest or working in the mills.

Kenneth Hunt

Occupationally, Cougars have found themselves working at one time or another in most of the following fields of
work:

Lumbering or woodcutting—in some phase of cutting down
    trees or transporting them or in the sawmill
Mining—digging, blasting, shoring up, etc.
Carnivals or fairs
Construction work—on reclamation or building projects
    setting up scaffolds, roofing, the "hard-hat" jobs
Cattle-ranch hand

Farm-labor work

Fishing, including shrimping, clamming, gathering mussels, diving for abalone

Oil-field and pipeline roustabout

Short-term kitchen help

Scavenging—working junkyards, wrecking, and hauling rubbish

General handyman

●      ●      ●

## MEL SETTLE

"I was up in Prairie City, Oregon. Picking cherries was over and bucking hay wasn't ready. This fellow came up to me and asked: 'Have you ever wrestled a bear?' *Have you ever wrestled a bear?* Seeing the man was the owner of a traveling show, and me needing money, my interest was ready. It would be a new experience. So I says, 'Why no, I haven't—who is she?' And do you know what?

He took me over and introduced me to this 350-pound, hairy, four-footed male, and before you know it we were at it.

"For me, it was kinda like instant learning. I grabbed his left paw and twisted it away from his body and he went down with me on top. . . . Later I found if I got ahold of his right paw and twisted to the left he'd go down too. Bears don't have the movement of the wrists, elbows or shoulders as we do, so when you twist against them, they fall quick to stop the pain.

"I wouldn't advise your trying it with a bear unless it was tame, for it does make the bear mad. Well, we traveled around with the bears to the little towns of Oregon, Nevada, Idaho, and Washington until it was time to go to Yakima and Wenatchee for the apples."

## THOMAS E. McANALLY

Tom is a family man and jack-of-all-trades. Trim, wiry, clear-eyed, his movements are relaxed and confident.

•          •          •

"I used to drive a logging cat, set chokers, be a head loader, feed a sawmill, weld, be a truck mechanic, a truck driver, a backhoe operator, run a dragline and a scrapper, a laborer, a fruit picker, and a cotton picker. Three months once my wife and the baby stayed in our car with a lean-to built off the side.

"We were picking fruit, but it kept raining a lot. But we didn't mind things too much.

"I've drove and handled just about any piece of machinery there is, and lately even been helping brand cattle.

"Been around a lot of men, and on the job they are the worst kind of cutthroat bastards that ever lived. But when off of the job they will pull their eye teeth for you. And I swore if ever I had the opportunity that I would start my own business and tend to it. And I didn't give a damn what it was, as long as it worked.

"So I tried selling Electrolux cleaners. Overall it was the worst. I was pretty damn sore.

"When a friend I had logged with called saying he needed help, I went to work for him.

"We were pulling a cable about three hundred feet up

a hill to pull the trees off. It was noon and we were tired and hungry. So I went to eat. He said anyone should be *the* able to put up with anything for eight hours. I said *hours* 'Yes, have you tried holding your breath for ten *are my* minutes, or holding an empty one-pound coffee *own* can at arm's length for ten minutes?' Then we came to work down here, and the owner of the ranch saw what the scoop was and gave me my first opportunity to start full time on my own. I had been cutting wood in my spare time before.

"And I found that cutting wood by myself, full time was better than any other job I've had. No breathing diesel smoke or redwood dust so damn thick you had to use the dozer to push it out of the way.

"I get a lot of exercise and all that. Sometimes not the right kind, but the hours are my own.

"I like to think I am giving a little to the community, both because of the need for energy and the need for cleared land for cattle. Not completely, though, for they need shade too. I leave a tree here and there.

"The Chinaman—what's his name—said, 'Your fault lies not in your technology or know-how but your lack of ambition.'"

## CHARLES "SLIM" RODGERS

Jack-of-all-trades, master of none, this Cougar tries his hand in the kitchen.

●    ●    ●

"This is the way I finally got here. I caught a bus to Sacramento hoping I could get a resort job and save some

money. So to Sacrameto I went and could go to
*work,* State Line to work, but it would have cost me all my
*work,* funds. So back to Frisco I went and borrowed more
*and* money and sold a pint of blood. Then back to Sac-
*work* ramento to buy another job. Well, I am working in
the kitchen of a work train. I know I am a long,
long way from Frisco, but the work and money I need. I
know I never expected to end up in this part of the world at
this time of life or even in the winter months. So here till I
leave or the train leaves to other places I work, work, and
work."

●         ●         ●

## ERIC FURBISH

"And then I got itchy feet again and thought oh heck I
gotta get outside. This inside work is killing me. I gotta get
out in that good sunshine and stuff where I
*gettin'* belong. I look like something that comes out of
*itchy* a sick bay. So I did. I quit. And by golly I knew a
*feet* guy who had a dad out there in the desert, and his
dad had a year lease on a gold claim. Well, that's
up my alley. And so I talked to him, and he says sure, come
on out there."

●         ●         ●

## MEL  SETTLE

"You put out a lot of good labor and get nothing for it.
They lie to you, too. They say they're paying $2.35 an hour
picking melons, and after you get out there they say the jobs

open are the short-handle-hoe jobs. And they pay $1.80 to $2.00. Then if you want to get back to town you have to pay $2.00 to take you back into town."

•          •          •

When working farm labor you are either on the day hauls or living at a farm labor camp. On the day hauls, you start very early in the morning and often have a better chance of making more money than when living in a camp. The cook at the camp probably doesn't get an early start in the morning, so you wait around for breakfast. The farm labor contractor doesn't charge anything for the day haul. He collects from the farmer himself for this service.

Although you're not paid for any driving time, you are paid for the time during the day it takes to be driven from one field to another. On some runs, there are coffee and wine stops, so it can take as much as two hours to get from Stockton to Patterson, fifty miles away.

The labor contractor lets onto the buses only those he wants, and often there is a kind of selective prejudice. Several fellows have told me that nowadays most of the farm labor contractors are of Mexican origin and favor Chicanos over whites and blacks. Thus, you can be down at 1:00 A.M. and still not be assured of getting on for a single day's work.

The contractor is paid two dollars a head for everyone he takes from town out to the camp. At the camp you perhaps can get two sandwiches and pop for about a dollar, and for fifty cents more you can eat a hot meal. And you pay around four dollars for the cot and eats for the night. So you owe for being taken out to the camp, for anything consumed along the way, and for your food and bed for the night. You owe all of this before you've had a chance to put in any work. Then the next day you might make twelve dollars and you'll be staying overnight paying another four to five dollars. So you're still broke. Well, in a couple more days, either you're disgusted or the work has run out. So back to town you go with little to show for the four or five days of tension and work.

Farm labor camps vary greatly, but as of 1973 a large one in Patterson was just a barn—no heat, no lights, just a plain cot. You may pay $4.00 for the cot and meal and 75 cents for the use of each blanket. Then you are out during the day chopping weeds in the sugar beets, making from $1.80 to $2.00 an hour.

Here's a two-day work experience in 1973:

### 9 hours

| | |
|---|---:|
| Regular | $18.00 |
| Board | 7.95 |
| Advance | .50 |
| S.D.I. | .18 |
| F.I.C.A | 1.05 |
| State | — |
| Withheld | 1.75 |
| | |
| Net pay | $6.57 |

Maybe the winos have a workable solution to their lives after all.

Here's something else. You can't get mad at the contractor because he'll call the sheriff and say you're "a trouble maker." Then the sheriff will tell you to get on down the road, or else he'll take you to jail. In such cases you won't be getting any money. The contractor can't say he won't pay you, but he's likely to say he'll send you the money. But hell, you've no address or place to receive it. And the contractor might say that you came out drunk, and maybe he will lie again and say you got paid when you didn't. Some fellows just feel disgusted and walk on down the road. And there's nothing much you can do about it unless you go to the labor commissions. Yet as one worker recently told me, "Now I think that you can complain to Chavez, and he'll send someone out to investigate."

As another Cougar commented: "There's nothing left but me. The way to get along is to go to the union hall or employment office and fill out an application. I've *nothing* been on the road for a couple of years and haven't *left but* much to fill in. They tell you, 'If we find some- *me* thing within the next couple of weeks, we'll let you know.' But with no address, no nothing, what is a fellow to do in the meantime? Jesus, after fifteen years I've not got anything. No money, no home, or anything."

And yet another: "So I go down and shoot at the employment office and see if I can do better. They ask for references. Can't give any as I've been a fruit tramp and off and on worked for a gyppo logger. They'll refer you back to the farm labor office, and that office will send you right back to the farm labor camp you started out at."

In 1966 a friend wrote from Stockton: "I told you one time about men working down here for $2.00 or $3.00 a day and I can show you right now. There are men here with familys that are working for that. If you don't believe me come down some day and go down there with me. But don't dress too good.

"Then you can talk to them and I don't mean the

tramps here I mean the family men. They fite to get on the buss'es. They are also on wellfare in the winter *they* which is now but they have to be for they can't *fite to* make it any other way with a family. Try to pay *get on* rent and feed a wife and child on that money. I *the* can't feed myself on $10.00 and live right now. *busses* Some that you see down there are white but most of them are not but they are amaricains. That is what I think."

Several years later this same man wrote from a labor camp next to the bridge just over the Salinas River on the road to Monterey.

"I thought I could find work here and save some money to find a place in Stockton for my wife and me. But I can see that I will never make it here for we are *I want* only getting in a few hours a week just enough to *to work* pay board and room and cigarettes. I will be *and save* lucky if I have $2.00 left over this pay day and we *some* only got in 3 hours today so it don't look too *money* good for this week eather. I am having hell just staying here in camp as most of the men here stay on the wine most of the time. I don't know where they get the money to drink on but there is 5 men drunk on it right now in our room. They can get drunk on two quarts of wine and that only cost a $1.50 so there is always some of them drunk and raising hell espeshaly the Nigro's. I was only able to get 4 hower's sleep last night as they talked and raised kane all night, so you can see I am having hell as I want to work and save some money. So I am going to try to get $30.00 together so I can get to southern California to prune grape as the weather won't bother me there and I can work every day but the frost and rain here has stop every thing and they don't know when it will start again. But they say it will be a month to two months as the frease has done too much damage. Some of the crops that are ready to harvest has been completely destroyed."

•          •          •

"Well, I thought I would drop you a line or two. I'm not doing any thing right now as the transmission is getting to bad to drive the car. So I had to quit the job I had for I had no way to get to it. I didn't mind so much for myself but I had 4 other men depending on me to get to work on the job so they lost out to.

"I have been to town the last five days and there isn't any thing down there but toping carrots and you just can't make any thing doing that. The top men don't *after* average $5.00 a day doing it but that isn't even *you buy* easy to get on as they only take a few people *lunch* and most of them work there every winter and *there* I don't think it's worth walking down there to *isn't* take that any way for after you buy lunch there *much left* isn't much left and it's 2½ mile to walk from here.

"I am afraid to drive the car if the transmission goes compleatly out I would have no way to get it back home. I do want to keep it for it does have a good motor in it, and I just put 2 tire's on it while I was working here so *sure gets* it will be worth it for me to put a transmission *tiresome* in it than to get another car but I guess I will *just* have to wait till next spring to get it fixed when I *lazing* can get work off the street here as there just *around* isn't any thing right now unless you have trans- *the house* portation to get on it and I was going to sign up in the trailer howse plant that they are opening up this month in Mantico but I will have to wait now till I can get the car fixed. I was going to go to Woodland to a plant I know there to try to get work but I knew that wouldn't work as I would be to close to Sacramento and before you knew it I would be trying to live with my wife again and there is to much tension in the house when I'm there for me to hold a steady job and when there is to much tension you know me I go to the bottle to relieve it and it only makes more the next day. I do still go see her and the kid's but it looks like that's all it can be now. Well other wise every thing here is fine. Dad is feeling better now than he has for several year and is gaining a little weight and we got a TV the other day while I was working so it dose give me something to do besides read but it sure getting tiresome just lazing around the howse and watching TV. I've been with out work now for 18 day's as I was afraid to drive the 25 miles with the car. Every thing was all right till I got stuck on the job one day and had to use the reverse a lot and I did know it was a little weak and it broke a seal and now it just porse out the fluid so the only thing I can do is wait and try to get a used one when I can get to work. For its not like it used to be here if you don't have transportation you just don't work steady. Well I will close for now.

P.S. I have looked in to it and it is going to cost me $75.00 for a good used transmission and about $5.00 for the back ruber seal and front gasget and then I can put it in my self or I can get a rebuilt transmission install for about $119.00 and I think the car is worth it so that is what I am going to do when I can save enough money. I am still going to try to find something soon but it doesn't look to good but at least it get's me out of the howse for three or four hr. every morning and the work does me good. I think I could of had the money to fix the car if I had known it was going to go out but insteade I put tire's on it and bought cloths that I needed mostly underwear and socks and was going to get new pants then the car went out at one's and that stoped that and I just blew up and drank the rest up for I only had about $18.00 left and I knew that wouldn't do any good any way and $10.00 of that I got when I took the other men out to get what they had coming and tell the farmer I couldn't work any more. I was only making $10.00 to $12.00 but that was better than nothing. Well I will close for now for sure. If you ever have Blue Chip stamps we could use them."

## O. LLOYD HICKS

A boyish vitality and happy-go-lucky spirit combine with rugged outdoorsy good looks. The West has been his beat for thirty years, and there's not much he can't do. Out of deference to his interest in the possibility of Cougars helping Cougars, he has acquired the nickname "T.C." (Top Cougar).

●          ●          ●

"You're lucky if you can average eight hours a day work for as long as a month. And what you get is about $1.50 an hour after deductions. Even for a single person this hardly gets you enough for the necessities of life. It's hard outdoor work and you're so tired in the evening that you can't go anywhere. Its hard to sleep at night in the camps— the fellows around you get noisy and drinking and you start in too.

"Your morale is low. Many of the people you're with are fouled up and are there just to stay out of jail. The

stopped up toilets and broken plumbing and dirt and flies
and mud kind of smear into you. If you want to get out, how
can you? You've actually got no money to leave the camp.
The wine and everything else at the camp costs too much.

"I wish more of the farmers would get interested in the
living quarters of their workers. But it's left to the labor
contractors and they're in it for the money. And
*anybody* they are the ones who control the jobs and
*have a* accordingly the workers. How do you com-
*rich* plain and still keep a job? You follow the crops
*uncle?* and are idle much of the time. But it hangs
out all around you, 'If you don't like it you can
leave.'

"One small step would be to see that the laws are enforced. Often the pieceworker doesn't receive the 80 percent
of the basic minimum wage. And its against the law for
wine to be sold in the camps. You get caught in the system
and there's no easy way out. Does anybody have a rich
Uncle?"

KENNETH HUNT

"Someone had built a fire and was boiling coffee when
my brother-in-law introduced me to the logging boss, a big
man with wide shoulders and a big smile. His name was Sid.
He told me to get some coffee and then he called to another
man and told him that I would be setting chokers for him.
In setting chokers you have a long chain hooked onto a D-
12 Caterpillar tractor or similar large vehicle, and at the
other end of the chain there is a large hook. You wrap the
chain around a log using the hook to make a loop choking
the log so that the Cat-man can pull it away. It's a fast job,
and it is dangerous because some of the big logs roll when

there is pressure and strain on the chain, and if you are standing too close it will roll over on you or sometimes the chain would break a link and would snap back like a whip and catch you in the head, chest, legs or arm. Anyway, the man Sid shook my hand and said we would get along fine which we did for about three weeks."

•       •       •

The seventies are very different from the thirties and forties.

## ERIC FURBISH

"They were called beaneries instead of mess halls. The name was a handdown from fellers of past years. They gave room and board also. We ate in a long hall and slept in cabins, with four guys and yourself on good beds. Those were real good beds. And just to know we weren't scroungers, we miners, they'd change the sheets twice a week; we'd change our blankets twice every two weeks. You could change them more if you wanted. Anyway, oh hell, there are no more places like these any more.

"Men can't get a job like I did, like I used to. Walk down the street and say you wanted work and get it. Be a *men can't* tramp-logger, a tramp-miner, anything. Or go *get a job* on down the road to the next place, and just go *like I* get work. Or go from one place to another with *used to* freedom in the air and the wind in your face. Too much union, too much insurance with medicals and X-ray exams. At that time you had X-rays of lungs for silicosis. That's from the silica dust underground. If you had it, well, you didn't get no job, and you coughed yourself to death eventually; and you couldn't get a job again with that silicosis. And the medical examinations of heart, breathing, reflexes and such, plus the most important was eye exams. Had to have damn good eye exams: twenty-twenty vision, no color blindness, or bad ears. They had to be in good condition also. And on top of all this now you must have X-rays of the small of your back for vertebrae slips or discs strained. Most all that has a bad back now are the young fellows. Yeah, they sure do. From playing sports in high schools and like that."

# 7

# Cougar Habitats—Jungles, Missions, Flophouses, and Parks

As I stood on the curb across the street from the group of men, my stomach began to contract from the sight of them. Even though I was one of them, I could never quite feel right about it. How pitiful they seemed to me. How terribly lonely and frightened some were. Most were standing with hands in empty pockets, stooped shoulders, head drooped down on chest, walking around in circles staring yet seeing nothing. I wanted to run away from them, to hide from them, never again to look at those faces with all those wrinkles and lines of hardship. I wanted to run because I was looking at myself across the street. It seemed to me we were just bodies moving without destination, save oblivion.

Kenneth Hunt

In any city and in many towns you can see them, sometimes singly and sometimes in groups: the drifters. In Sacramento, in the park almost in the shadow of the state capitol, you may have seen some of them playing dominoes. In Stockton you may have hurried past the workingmen's hotels—the Wolf, the Earle—which you know have seen different, though not necessarily better, days. The drummers and salesmen are now staying in aseptic motels, each of which is bright and clean and just like thousands of others all across the land. In Fresno or San Jose or at St. Anthony's in San Francisco, there are lines of them forming at mission doors, often half awake, eyes staring. You may try to avoid them as if they don't exist. But if you look at them because they do exist, they appear unclean and infected with unknown contagions. If you are of the Protestant ethic, you may dismiss them as being shiftless, lazy, and unwilling to work. You see them not working, so you feel it is their fault. People get what is coming to them.

Yet you're driving down a street in Modesto or just off the mall in Fresno and see the outsiders, and something within you whispers that were it not for the inherited farm, the uncle who put you through school, or your rich wife, you might be there standing and looking, standing and looking.

Yesterday was yesterday. Today we eat; tomorrow we'll be out looking. That is the drifters' life. Hard work. Irregular work. Strains and injuries. Most of the rest of us, bloating with food and drink, sitting before our TV sets, are insensitive to all of this.

There is a whole other meaning to sweat—sweat that comes from physically grueling work rather than from the games and recreations at resorts and tennis clubs—and tears from agony that is real, not induced through momentary involvement in some drama or sad, sad song. There is a different meaning to blood that brings five dollars a pint, so that you can keep going—not the once-a-year contribution of a pint at a society benefit for a hospital's blood bank.

Where do the Cougars and their fellow drifters live? Not in the homes that you and I know, not in the subtopias, but in places where taxes rarely are a concern.

## THE PARKS

For a few minutes, imagine you're a thirsty drifter. You're forty, still healthy, and free from most of society's conventions. You have come out of a farm labor camp after a couple of weeks with all of twenty or maybe thirty dollars. So you're going to live it up a bit. You get off the day-labor bus and head on down for a beer and to listen to some shit-kicking music. You feel warmth toward those cowboys and cowgirls who got the old manure flying around the barns and raised country music into the mainstreams of America.

The day is still young, so it's on down to a honky-tonk where the women hang out. You have a night of it, and the next day you find yourself in the downtown park. The trees are massive, the shrubs flourishing, the benches handy, and there are restrooms so you don't have to go into a nearby bar. You run your fingers into your pocket which you know is empty except for the paper napkin serving as a handkerchief. You get to feeling like a bottle. So you have to find someone to put the rigging on. And after a couple of bummings you feel better, for you've made your hit.

The day drags on, and you're talking with some of the other fellows—observations on the world, your stint in the military, families of long ago, and the lousy conditions at the labor camps.

Someone is getting up a Frisco circle, and you want to be a part. The guy is shouting in a weak voice, "OK you tramps. I've got two bits; my partner here has the same. Dig deep, and get the Frisco on the road." Five cents, fifteen, seven cents, it comes in. And the money is counted, and a wino is sent to make the run to the store. There are six of you together who made up the circle, but a seventh fellow has edged in. He's a hobo trying to horn in even though he hasn't contributed. A tramp can spot a hobo as easily as he can spot a plainclothesman or a phoney. If that hobo takes a drink and the tramps notice, someone will be on the sidewalk, in jail, or in a hospital that night.

If it's true that people are enhanced by their environments and come to reflect them, then the person who spends hours each day in some park must be an enriched human. It's not just a matter of playing checkers or dominoes or bullshitting. It is a matter of social intercourse, sharing and experiencing, and accepting and being accepted. Friendly advice is given, and you listen to the concerns of others. High in the buildings surrounding the park the psychiatrists and other professionals are providing similar services for those who want to learn to live with themselves and their families—all within four decorated walls.

In Stockton a matronly woman would come down to the Plaza Park with a basket of sandwiches. If there was a Cougar about, he invariably tried to "protect" her, insisting that the fellows didn't use vulgar language in her presence. The woman would say no one should take more than two sandwiches so that they would go around. But it got to the point that the bums would stuff their pockets and then fights started, and the police had to tell the woman not to come to the park any more. "I never went for vulgar language around women. I knocked a couple fellows down, and then the police came," is the way one Cougar explained the incident.

In Stockton a bakery used to give out free bread, and a dairy in Modesto offered milk shakes in a can. Borden's in Merced let you have broken cartons of milk. Down in San Jose, a candy company used to give out sacks of candy. But some of the winos started hawking these items down the street, and for public-health reasons among others, the handouts were stopped.

## MISSIONS

In the middle 1930s, I was about to bed down under a bush on the Boston Common when someone whose face I didn't see said, "Kid, you will be rousted if you stay here. Go on down to the Staniford Street Mission near the North Station. With your youth and suitcase and all, they might let you sleep there. But move on, move on."

At the mission, fellows were already being turned away. The religious service was over, and there was a limited number of sleeping cots upstairs. A man who seemed quite ancient to me at that time (now I know he must have been all of fifty) was the unpaid in-residence supervisor. He was called "Pop." When he announced, "Full up," then saw my disappointed face, he added, "Come in and I'll find you a place." And he did. Later I learned that it was his cot I had slept in and that he made do in a rocking chair.

This was a good mission, in some ways the best I've ever known. About a dozen of us could stay there at night while we were sorting ourselves out and deciding what we'd do or where we would head next.

I had an old shirt, torn and missing some buttons which I offered to the only other relatively young man there. The wife of the mission preacher observed this and quietly told me, "You know it's nice of you to offer your shirt, but sometimes the gift is not worth the giving." And to this day I remember her words and watch the quality of my giving.

One evening, feeling my oats and finding that the in-housers were supposed to give testimonials to show what the Lord had done for them and how salvation was working, I found myself on my feet up front, lustily adding my bit: "Am I Jesus' little lamb? Yes, you're God damned right I am!" "Pop" and the rest all knew that this would have to be farewell. There was less than the usual conversation before we went to our cots that night.

In the morning, still cocky, though a little sheepish, I went down to the table off the kitchen for early-morning breakfast. If you had a job or were actively looking, you ate at 6:30. Otherwise, it was 7:00. And considering that most of the food came from nearby restaurants or from baskets brought from churches, the 6:30 chow was somewhat more varied. At least you had a sporting chance for wieners.

About nine of us were at the early chow, and as I was close to finishing, Pop placed a slice of apple pie in front of my plate. I waited, but there was just that single slice, with no other slices appearing. It just wasn't big enough to start quartering or the like. And I got to noticing that I was being unobtrusively watched by each of the men. And Pop was standing by the stove with the coffee pot and smiled a bit when I turned his way. I was the "kid," and they had some-how got me a piece of pie. And I was to eat that pie.

So I took my fork and reached forward, and my wrist involuntarily trembled. I swallowed hard and made another pass in the direction of the pie, and my whole arm jerked. I felt I was a tough kid, scared of nobody or nothing, as I had been telling myself all summer. But I couldn't pick up that piece of pie. My eyes and nose began to moisten, and I was near to giving out with some primal scream. But I knew the pie had to be eaten. The men wanted it. I wanted it. All had to be pleased.

Letting go of my fork, both hands shot out to that piece of pie, and I put it into my mouth. Gulping and half gagging, I got it down. And I looked up, and they were all watching. Some smiling, others with moistened eyes, too. I got out of my chair, mumbled something, and left the mission in body but never in spirit.

So missions mean much to me. The Pajaro Rescue Mission at Watsonville Junction and the Victory Mission in nearby Salinas have given much satisfaction. Missions are great stopping-over places, though usually you're limited to a night or two at most, and the capacity is rarely equal to the demand. There is usually an hour's service, often given by earnest, scrubbed teenagers, living well away from the area of lo-ball, pan, poker games, and hockshops. Fine kids, though most haven't as yet had much time to observe, let alone live. They tell you about how much Christ means to them. You can just picture their having prayed to pass their last school exam. Nice young folks, and certainly better in many ways than many of their elders who have sold out to antihumanistic forces in society.

There's the good soup or stew and bread, generally enough for a most welcome meal. Then, built up with thoughts of a better life or kingdom up there somewhere and with a satisfied stomach, the door opens, and to the strains of an exit march, perhaps "Onward Christian Soldiers," you head on out onto the cold sidewalk. Now you've got to scrounge around to find a place to lie down for the night. You were warm inside when you came out: the buildup, and now the letdown.

One blustery, wintry night, a fairly young Cougar was leaving the service at the San Jose Rescue Mission and heading for nearby St. James Park, across from the Hotel St. James. Slowly he read the Mission's large sign: "For the wages of sin is death, but the gift of God is eternal life through Jesus Christ our Lord (Romans 6:23)." To no one in particular he said, "Meet me in the park, O Lord. Meet me in the park. We can tell each other a few things."

An aging Cougar reminisced, "So you go to these missions. Ninety percent are there for the food only. Some fellows in there looking for something better. Ought to be more than just a cup of food and turning out into the cold again. No bed, or prospects of a bed, no nothing. Won't even make a phone call for you in most of them. That one in Modesto wouldn't, . . . This deaf-mute wanted to go out in the country where they knew him, but a call had to be made so they would come and get him. I didn't have any money so I went down to the sheriff and he made the call. They came and got him, this mute."

The preacher or father in charge of a mission has to make ends meet. In order to obtain broad church, individual, and organizational support, he adopts many kinds of stereotypical behavior. Sometimes he has to yield to well-intended pressures.

To get a night's sleep at a mission, it is common practice to require identification and a Social Security number. You have to sign in. And if you have lost your Social Security card and you've never replaced your wallet since it was stolen years ago, what can you do? And if you happen to have picked one up off the sidewalk or if you gave someone a dollar for a wallet with cards and names in it, you can't hazard using the phony ID card. For you run the risk of signing the name of a fellow running from the law. And when you're picked up, you're really in a peck of trouble. But worse is the fact that the missions aren't open in the daytime. Law and order and religion and the merchants must not be offended. What is a man to do from 7:00 A.M. to 6:00 P.M.? The mission doesn't want to annoy the good people of the community who don't like to see groups of drifters or the poor congregated in any single area. How many of those who say drifters should be working during the day do their part to provide jobs?

## JUNGLES

Santa Rosa, California, is unusual in having an urban jungle. Many people live within two hundred yards of it, and thousands of people must pass by each day, almost all unaware of the high low-life a few feet away. In front of the train station is a small park with an enormous monkey tree and several other large trees that flourish in this one-time hometown area of Luther Burbank, the plant breeder. On most any sunny afternoon, a half-dozen drifters are sunning themselves, some waiting to go out on the next freight, others sticking around to work at some casual labor. Up the block is a liquor store, and across the street is the Rescue Mission, where you might get a flop for the night after first putting up with the Jesus shouting.

A block apart are two workingmen's hotels, one with girls available for night duty, the other for serious drinking and a little dancing. Alongside one of these establishments are thick shrubs, carefully fenced. In this small rectangular maze is a minijungle.

Water is available, toilet facilities can be had by going in the side door to the bar, minimal warming is possible, but an open fire is unwise. And there's some privacy for lying down and sleeping. The tops of the wooden rails on the fence are worn where bodies have struggled up and over. And in the fall the dusty, unripe grapes shine where eager fingers have probed them. Behind the building are sheets of cardboard, ready to be carried back into the enclosure.

Can we assume that the urban-renewal zealots will catch up with this jungle and self-righteously destroy yet another habitat of the working tramp, drifter, wino, and Cougar? Across the tracks, in the high weeds next to some discarded junk, used to be another jungle. Now a chain-link fence encircles this area with only the property owners or workers able to enter.

More than one Cougar has used such a stopover point while waiting to get on as a dairy hand or a fruit or grape picker or help someone load or unload a truck. The ware-housemen or teamsters getting six dollars or more an hour often don't mind giving a fellow a dollar or two for doing all of the loading.

"Have you been in San Bernardino?" asked a Cougar. "There's a guy up there, a rich man with a big mansion setting up by the mountain there in San Berdoo, and he's got back of his house a great big yard which used to be lawn and shrubbery. He lets these hobos and tramps and Cougars and whomever build little shacks on that property. If a guy doesn't have any money or if there isn't room in one of the shacks for him, he'll send a man with a note to the lum-beryard so he can get enough lumber to build his own. The fire department got after this rich guy, who then got five-gallon garbage cans with stovepipes hanging out of them to satisfy basic cooking requirements. This fellow often sleeps in a shack even though he's got that mansion."

During the 1930s a woman lived at Santa Barbara, just after the train starts slowing from Montecito. There were all kinds of huts there. Once a year she made everyone clear out and apologized for doing it. She would bring food and other things to make it easier, saying that it had to be done to conform to the law. She didn't call us squatters, but we understood. She was a great lady. I think there's a children's zoo there now.

When I was a boy in the jungles of the West, old-timers told tales about a Mrs. Parrott who lived on the peninsula south of San Francisco. For several decades around the turn of the century, she would feed any drifter who came by. It took a special cook to feed the men and women (as many as a hundred, sometimes) who would show up at her "Baywood" estate. Many camped nearby for a night or two.

Sacramento is still surrounded by several jungles. One of the most important is now the no-man's-island in an area in the bottom of the American River, about a mile from the state fairgrounds. There are water and facilities for cooking and camping, although not up to most vacationers' standards.

At Broderick, across the I Street bridge is another flat land, and it is very livable. On up at Roseville, where there is a major railroad switching yard; up to thirty fellows can be seen scavenging the dump. Not too many miles north, at Oroville, there is a rail division point where boxcars are repaired; a mile and a half down the track there's a good place far enough out of town for the city cops not to bother you and where the railroad guys let you be.

Marysville had a great jungle in the river bottoms. But

the deaths of so many who stayed there brought in the police, who cleaned the men out. Among those who know the scene, there is no hostility toward the police. For there were over twenty-five graves found of drifters last seen in the company of Corona or his brother. And there are countless tales of waking up in the bushes and seeing a dark figure hurrying away.

The best jungles are those not too far from major railroad yards, where there's a good source of water and pans and large cans left along with some eating utensils for whoever comes by. Also, there needs to be a protected area to cook in and have a small fire that won't ignite anything on a wintry night. Until recently, many a hobo would stay over for a while in a jungle and serve as a camp tender. He would do the cooking, clean the utensils, and watch the bedrolls of those out on jobs.

"The Cougar can adjust to any situation, and he's satisfied eating his food out of cans by a smoky outdoor fire to a neatly decorated dining room, sleeps in a boxcar or on cold, hard ground as well as on a new waterbed. He can bathe in the icy waters of a canal or river or in hot or cold water of a bedroom. He does these things without worry or complaint. His philosophy is that of saying 'Let the chips fall where they may, who cares?'"

Kenneth Hunt

Inexpensive hotels, bunkhouses, flophouses, missions, boxcars, parks, jungles, and even caves are lodgings for the American drifter. Boxcars are generally used only when traveling. The way things are these days, you can hardly get sleep, for there is always the worry that someone might come upon you in the dark and not only roll you but perhaps kick you off the moving train.

The flophouses like those on West Madison Avenue in Chicago, Larimer Street in Denver, and in Los Angeles and Eureka, are becoming scarcer. The bunk, sometimes separated from others by plywood and chicken wire over the top, is not too bad a place, but it is frowned on by most anyone who prefers sleeping in a trash bin or under a bush on a cold night.

The politicians, developers, city planners, and urban-renewal proponents have banded together to tear down inexpensive housing, all the while talking about better living quarters to come.

Yet in destroying the little bit of community that drifters have established and in forcing them outside of the routines of the more settled skid rowers and pensioners, they have left the drifters with no congenial place, with nothing at all. And the unions, through the building codes, make sure that simple, decent housing is unavailable.

So the drifters choose between nights in the Salvation Army, missions, boxcars, the weeds, or perhaps a few days at a farm labor camp, and then a night in a workingmen's hotel, where at least there's a TV set. These drifters are hardly thought of as having basic human needs. Public housing is for the city indigents, the stay-putters, those who cry out against their lot.

# Family Life and Marriage

I can't support my socks, let alone a wife.

My mother always told me not to take the last piece of bread.

A Cougar turning down the<br>last cigarette in the pack

My footprints are back there in Oklahoma, but I won't ever go back to fill them.

A Cougar leveling with himself

He'd love you with all his heart and he'd break you with all his heart. That's the kind of guy he was.

Widow of a Cougar

Not long ago a Cougar, when asked what kind of a woman he would like to have as a wife, replied, "The regular kind. . . . It doesn't make much difference whether she is good or bad because I figure that either way a fellow could make a good woman out of a bad one, or a bad one out of a good one. . . . I mean bad in the sense that she has problems. How serious these problems will become depends on you. . . . All women I believe like to be treated real nice, not just by material things but personally. Most fellows tend to pick wives largely on a sexual basis, but for me complete companionship is primary. I want to share and be proud with her, and I have to keep in mind that material things aren't going for me. The feeling behind is what counts."

Generally speaking, Cougars want marriage to be a total commitment. Sex as sex has been relatively easy to come by, particularly around the hotels and bars, and accordingly, sex does not become justification for marriage. I've yet to hear a Cougar boast about sexual conquests or brag about seductions.

## WOMEN

If you're over twenty and your life doesn't include going to classes, attending church, participating in office parties, spending afternoons on the golf links or evenings playing cards at the Elks or Moose, just where are you likely to meet women? The women you do meet are in lobbies, at a bar, or on the street, and many of them are there on account of being serious drinkers, hustling for one-night stands, or being unhappy about their private lives.

The strongly woman-motivated Cougar all too often finds himself "protecting" some woman in the bar. "Cool

it! You can't talk that way here . . . a lady's present," he
might say to any male patron using expressions like "For
God's sakes!" or "Screw it!" If the woman feels the need
for attention, when a fellow down the bar has done nothing
more than look hopefully in her direction, she might
announce to one and all, "He's insulting me!" The Cougar
falls for the bait, filled with a desire to defend womanhood
in general as well as this one woman in particular.

Hours of togetherness follow in a booth alongside the
wall, in which the lonely Cougar finds himself admired for
his forcefulness. Here has been a social situation with which
he was able to deal effectively. It is no surprise when, in a
matter of hours or days, he has moved in with the woman.

Frequently, he finds out later that the woman whom he
"protected" encourages this repetitious behavior pattern.
She eggs him on into barroom verbal and physical fights.
She insists that he ask his boss for a raise even though he
has held the job only for a month. Feeling uneasy about the
overall situation, he may take flight or he may accelerate his
drinking, get into a senseless fight, and find himself in jail.
The speed of his being bailed out is then in his wife's hands.
Thus, new marital discord develops.

The Cougar's view seems to be that a woman is to be
respected whether she has what are considered desirable
social habits or not. She may be a prostitute, hooker, or
hustler. She may be foul-mouthed, neglect her children,
and drink too much. Yet no man is a man if he uses abusive
language to her or about her to another man. She is part of
womanhood, like your mother or sister, and is entitled to
respect and protection.

As one Cougar put it to me upon his release from a jail
stint for fighting, "It's not the words, it's the implication.

It's what they're saying this girl *is*. If she is a whore, she knows it, and it's nobody's business. They're just trying to make her cry."

This inability to set the same standards for women and men, or to see men and women as equivalent, is a common Cougar characteristic. We can also sense that his attitude towards women is a kind of substitute for a religion. Womankind is essentially pure and holy: one need not understand, simply take it on faith. With this in mind it is easier to understand the Cougar's domestic life.

## MARRIAGE

Women who marry Cougars are usually in for a few surprises. For one, the armor of the knight sometimes tarnishes rather easily. Being manly doesn't necessarily include coming home for meals on time, maintaining routines, meeting payments, or changing any basic habit patterns. Well-furnished rooms, new gadgets and appliances, happy relationships with neighbors, car pools for the children, insurance policies, and planning for the future are incomprehensible to the Cougar, though he may find their newness interesting for a while. He doesn't see the value in having many changes of trousers; he's only wearing underwear to please his wife in the first place.

Ordinarily, marriage is thought of as a relationship, the cornerstones of which are reliability, perseverance, concern for family status, and long-term planning. Just where is there room for the Cougar in this scheme of things? It's almost like trying to make someone who is only visual minded into a professional musician. On the other hand, some Cougars are making it, but in these instances the wife supplies some subtle leadership and sees to it that there is continuity, that bills get paid, that the children get to school, and that house payments are met. In such instances, some of these arrangements are happy and lasting.

It may be that there is a sense of sharing of family responsibilities. Cougars do not insist upon being the head of the family in all respects, although they feel guilty if they are not good providers. They firmly believe that the man should be a good provider. When the woman takes on some of the other family responsibilties, the chances for marital success are much greater.

In a way, many people are guided by their ideas of what they "should" be. That is, the *idea* of self-image or role becomes more important than the behavior. You're supposed to have a circle of friends and do things with them. It is good to be a good mother or father, to keep your children immaculate and popular with their peers, and to have a wife who looks attractive to the other people in the community.

These ideas are rarely, if ever, apparent in either the conversations or the lives of Cougars. Occasionally, they may live with a spouse or someone with some of these values, and invariably, the Cougar is made to feel guilty and wonder about his own suitability as a spouse. He doesn't deny the merit of his spouse's viewpoint, and while supposedly thinking it over, he does more than an ordinary amount of running around. This only confirms the wife's feeling that he doesn't really love her enough to change his ways. A long series of temporary separations follows, and while neither husband nor wife really wants a divorce, they still are not able to live together in harmony for a prolonged period.

## CHILDREN

It's refreshing in a society in which smiling and gesturing at babies and young children so often isn't considered manly to see Cougars doing just that. A cockeyed smile, a few moments of peek-a-boo, and a reassuring rumpling of a child's head of hair come naturally. As one fellow put it about children, "They like recognition, too." The Cougar carries this awareness of and sensitivity to the feelings of the very young throughout his life.

It shows up in his spontaneity and in his discovery of newness in each experience. He gives to a child not in order to receive but because the child has a need and he enjoys responding to it. He may also be dimly aware of the child in himself.

Eric Furbish told me of an experience that reveals the child in him: "Once I found this big old hunk of quartz with a big gold streak running through it. Actually I had a few of them. You could split them and they'd come open so nice. I was going to sell them to jewelers for display in their windows. Then people would come along and see this beautiful piece of gold quartz and get their attention caught and be looking at the rest of the stuff in the window. Well, I had this one really big piece, and I put it up on top of the refrigerator. And this little Indian girl, about seven, a friend of mine, came in and I told her not to touch that one, that she could have any of the other ones, but not to touch that big one. She was going to school and her class was doing a rock collection. Well, I went off for a couple of days, and when I came back, it was gone. I was kind of mad at first, but the more I thought about it, the more I liked it—the thought of that little girl bringing that huge hunk into class for her rock collection. She must have gotten A-A-A- on that.

Everybody must have asked where'd you get it, where'd you get it? 'From my uncle.' Where'd *he* get it? 'Oh, he has a mine out in the desert somewhere.' I got a kick out of that. I never did get it back. That probably ended the rock collections right there. They probably went on to collecting flowers after that."

Cougars invariably love their children, and no matter what a child's appearance, they see it warmly, as a wonderful creation. This great interest in his children is something other than possessive, and it isn't even important for the child to be responsive. The Cougar sees the child as blameless and in need of tenderness. Only in the adult world is there wrongdoing and sin, both of which seem to have become institutionalized into the fabric of our culture.

When there are children, the Cougar who has ranged off and has possibly saved a couple hundred dollars will as often as not send it to his woman to buy something for the kids or show up himself and take them out to buy school clothes for the fall or Easter outfits or elaborate Christmas toys, possibly a small backyard polyethylene swimming pool. "I love my children," he will say, completely oblivious that if he had used the couple hundred dollars to join a construction laborer's union, he might be in a position to provide for their economic well-being more regularly. It is the wife who is left to suffer from his lack of planning.

Generally, Cougars use expressions in their family life, such as "I'd like to do that," "you want to do that?" but not the expression "Let's us do that." Seldom is there a suggestion of joint action with another person, whereas the wife quite often makes suggestions that he obligingly follows and often thoroughly enjoys. With a few exceptions, his enjoyment is not in long-term planning or studying but in the immediate responsiveness and happiness of other persons.

When one Cougar, whose parents had been divorced some years earlier was asked what the basis of their divorce had been, he replied, "I don't know. I never thought about it. Why know the reason? They're them and I'm me and what they do is theirs to do." This man at long intervals sees both of his divorced parents separately and is content to let it go at that.

A Cougar whose daughter was in high school—the roving ways of her family had resulted in her being in more than fifteen schools already—jilted a boyfriend who subsequently bad-mouthed her around the school. The father took immediate action, beating up the boy and his older brother on the basis that it was his fatherly responsibility to look out for his daughter. He gave no thought to the possibility of injuries to the boys, a lawsuit by the boys' family, the chance of being thrown in jail, or injury to himself. When these risks were pointed out to him, he looked puzzled and said, "But wouldn't you do the same?"

The uncomplaining Cougar is usually kind in a face-to-face way to his wife and children. Living in the present, however, he fails to realize how much one human affects another. Marriage is an interconnection between human beings. The inability of either mate to stand in the other's shoes leads to the shifting of marital feet.

# Cougarish Personal Attitudes

Life's a game if you have a stadium.

I like to depend on myself.

The more uptight and crooked a person is, the more likely he'll be demanding that people be square shooters.

Merchants operate on other people's money.

Money is an instrument to obtain things you want.

The thing you get means more than the money, or you wouldn't be spending it on it.

Look before you leak. The guy next to you may be barefooted or have holes in his boots, or be a midget.

If a Cougar does too much thinking without constructivity, he gets to drinking to blank out his mind.

On what do you bias your opinion?

Words make certainty possible, but reality doesn't.

A Cougar cannot stand pressure like the real four-legged cougar can't stand being caged. Both need to be free in action, feelings, and decisions. He will often listen to suggestions but will in the end do his own thing.

Conversations with Cougars

When you're not closely tied to religion, church, school, political party, clubs, organizations, occupation, family, or sense of duty, and when you are not bursting with ideas of social reform, it's easier for the world to be your oyster. In return for not trying to impose rigid standards of behavior on others, you wish to be treated the same way—to be left alone to do as you please. After all, a human is a human, and the great big, wide, wonderful world belongs to each and every one of us. This general approach cuts down a great deal of personal and social flak. There may be internal gnawing about one's past, but there's always the present, and one day at a time is enough.

Although aware of some personal shortcomings, Cougars tend to feel at ease with themselves and to accept others. On the whole, they are pleased that their shortcomings aren't any greater than they are. They think of individual persons, not of people in the abstract. They do not want individuals whom they know to suffer "dis-ease."

Not given to extremes in talking about themselves, they rarely brag about past exploits. You don't find them telling about the medals they've won, how many women they laid in a single night, how many rich or notorious friends they have had, or how fast they drove between Topeka and Denver. If a Cougar works on a 10,000-acre cattle ranch, he's unlikely to mention that his employer comes and goes in a twin-engine Cessna. You're more apt to hear about the ranch equipment or some odd rock or cloud formations that he saw. People in his working environment are accepted as people, not as social curiosities or types to be labeled.

Neither rebel nor conformist, he is saddled with his own convictions, most of which make sense, or at least seem to, until measured by the ways of society at large.

Saying that the Cougar lacks a personal philosophy is a misunderstanding. His philosophy is based on the fundamental needs and truths of equality and freedom. Of course, people are different. Let them be different. That is their way. Who are we to manipulate another, even for personal gain? This expression of independent, nonevaluative enjoyment of the present is something wonderful to behold—especially when the restrictions and restraints of civilization have not completely straitjacketed the individual.

However, Cougars, like most of us, have certain prejudices. Some of the more common ones are intellectuals, or people who live in a world of words and think that the verbal world is more important than the nonverbal world. Other prejudices might include unclean hippies; young men who let themselves be taken care of by young women; people who would tell you what to do and what not to do; politicians; drug pushers; homosexuals; people who don't keep their word; people who mistreat women; farm labor contractors.

## THE MANIPULATORS

Cougars view the world as being run by powerful cliques in big business and big labor who are in cahoots with the politicians. These groups maintain their power, positions, and profits by encouraging wars. The evidence, Cougars seem to feel, is in what the politicians do and not in what they say. They may even feel that the outcome of elections is determined ahead of time by the deliberate selection of a weak candidate to oppose someone that "they" want to be elected.

One Cougar put it this way: "I've never voted for anything because I've never really cared about who runs for this or that office. What they do or don't do doesn't bother me one bit. Voting is good if a guy wants to take part in it, to try to help the man he wants into office. But my opinion is that the results of not voting are the same because I think that the man for a public office is already picked and has the job long before the vote takes place."

This skepticism toward those in control of most institutions of society has many ramifications. For one thing, it provides sound grounds for not fitting into institutional procedures. It helps justify living instinctively without feeling obligated to adopt imitative styles. Quite obviously, if the demons in the world are out there and not within, then it's much easier to feel comfortable with and about oneself.

As for promotion, advertising, and selling in general, the Cougar is almost totally disenchanted. At least institutionalized commercialism is outside of his interests. Those who manipulate words and images and play on pleasant associations to get people to buy things they don't really need live in a totally different world. The Cougar can't see how any cream, lotion, or substance could possibly be smeared on the face of a girl to add to her radiant beauty. Buying kitchen gadgets and appliances to fit a decor strikes the Cougar as strange and even funny.

What happier kitchen is there than one where the baking odors are leaking out of the oven door and where it's warmer near the stove than across the room? I've rarely met a Cougar who didn't prefer a wood stove to an elaborate range, who didn't find elemental satisfaction in chopping or sawing wood and feeding the fire.

## LADY LUCK

"It's the way the dice fall." "What do you mean the deck is stacked; I slipped in my own cards." "Nature's just one big lottery." "Mother Nature and Lady Fortune won't just hand you anything. You must use your body strength to receive what you want." One Cougar sat by a jukebox feeding coins to hear over and over again "The Wheel of Fortune." Yet as far as I can tell, Las Vegas, Reno, and Tahoe are no more likely to be Cougar centers than Ogden, Bakersfield, and Tucson.

Challenges are to the Cougar's liking. He often figures that he might be "lucky" and win. If someone bends an old-fashioned, tough, beer-bottle cap between his thumb and index finger, the Cougar is likely to assume he can, too. He may even bet that he can bend a second cap between his second and third fingers at the same time. The newness in this untried task increases his interest in trying and helps compensate for his probable failure.

I remember one Cougar who, seeing a fellow lift the rear end of a Volkswagen, bet a quart of booze that he could lift the end of a Fordson tractor even though he had never tried. To the surprise of everyone present, he did it. Then he dropped the tractor and promptly fell writhing onto the ground because he had strained some tendons. Yet later on he felt it had been worth it to him. Challenge and luck can be an irresistible combination.

The Cougar is given to remembering his cutting eight cords of firewood or picking eighty dollars' worth of cherries in a single day. He thinks of the exception and not the average. You will run across him cheerfully pursuing some quest for buried treasure or a lost mine. Or he may be salvaging some kind of ship or truck wreck or just checking out some stream bed in the hope of finding nuggets of gold. Adventure, challenge, and luck all seem to be intertwined. Who knows when you might make the lucky strike, clean up at poker, or have the big day.

It is my suspicion that if luck were a gentleman, fewer Cougars would have faith in it.

## THE AGED AND DEATH

"Look at those ruts in his face. What a life he's led," observed a Cougar of an elderly man who in some quarters would be called a derelict, but not by any Cougar. Cougars see something to be admired in the aged that is quite different from any individual quality. Perhaps what they see in those ruts is evidence of having survived many days, one at a time, days in which it is as possible to meet one's end through one of the four horsemen of the Apocalypse as it is to be exterminated by the automobile or hardening of the arteries.

I've seen remarkable instances of individuals facing up to almost inevitable death. Jim Greer was such a man. Intelligent, commanding in presence, he was a thoroughly considerate gentleman. After the breakup of his marriage, he spent years drifting about the West and the South. He might winter on a cattle ranch in Montana or Nevada or along the Gulf of Mexico. If the latter, he would work his way northward, ending with the apple harvest in Washington in September and October. One fall day, realizing that he had been coughing blood day after day, he foresaw his own end. Stiffening himself with liquor, he went down to the tracks. The sheriff's report stated that he was hit by a train at the edge of town.

Memories are kept alive in many ways. Between the Western Pacific and Southern Pacific tracks near the lookout tower in Stockton there is a little slough with willows and tules. For years a hobo called it home—a couple of pans and plenty of cardboard for a mattress, with newspapers and brown wrapping paper for blankets and sheets. He would share his mulligan with passing drifters. If it rained, the railroad yardmen he cheerfully greeted each day would let him into a boxcar.

One day his body was found with his head bashed in.

The railroad men put up a little cross beside this smallest of jungles, where the pots still remain. It is the most moving grave I know.

## GIVING PRAISE AND BLAME

Cougars do not believe in the traditional Protestant morality of giving praise only when it is merited. Kind words are not limited in amount and need not be hoarded, they feel.

A Cougar with whom I was drinking coffee told the waitress, "That's delicious coffee." I was having trouble forcing myself to drink the stuff, so I asked him, "Do you really think this is good coffee?" He reflected for a moment and said, "Why, no, but you don't lose something by giving praise, and, you know, people are snobbish and a waitress appreciates any kind comment. You don't lose something by showing appreciation." What a difference this is from the common critical practice of expecting a certain level of quality or performance. Praise, for most people, is not something spontaneously given but a kind of reward for exceptional service. We forget that people need praise and that there may be something sinful in the common view, "If you weren't doing it right, I would have told you."

I remember pressing a point with a Cougar and being put back into the human race with, "You're doing fine— Sarge."

## SEX

Respect for women is universal among Cougars. Words such as "little" applied to a two-hundred-pound woman convey the kind of emotional rather than factual way that

Cougars respond to females. Women need protection so that they won't hurt themselves falling off the pedestals on which they've been placed—at least part of the time. Nevertheless, while they feel, in a sense, that men and women are equal, the Cougar would agree with the League of Women Voters, which until recently opposed the Equal Rights Amendment on the basis that many labor laws protect women and should be maintained.

Few things upset most Cougars more than the whole protective system surrounding pimps. A pimp is no good and should be treated as such by the powers that be. Little wonder that there is widespread lack of respect for the leniency and wisdom of the courts. This deep involvement runs contrary to the usual live-and-let-live approach of the Cougar. The difference may lie in the fact that many girls are not exercising free choice in their careers as prostitutes. The pimp who provides the apartment and fancy clothes also lets the girl know that not only will these be taken away from her if she doesn't hustle enough tricks and turn over the money but also that he will report her to her family back home and let them know what a bad girl she has been.

A revealing account of a prostitute and Cougar down on his luck bears retelling.

"It had been quite a while that I had had a sexual relationship with a girl, so when I sold my blood for five dollars, I thought that it would be pretty good to have a sexual release and at the same time help some girl out by giving her the money. So I went to a cathouse somewhere in Modesto.

"I told the madame I only had five dollars and that's it, no more, and she told me to go on back and talk to one of the girls and see if she would do anything.

"I saw this skinny girl—Carrie—and felt she needed

money the most. She was a good but mixed-up girl. I told her the truth about having only five dollars, that I wasn't working but needed to have a sex release to clear my mind. Carrie said that she understood and asked me to stay for a while, which I did. After a few hours I had to leave. This girl would not take the five dollars even though she would have to make it up to the house. Instead she gave me seven dollars, all she had in her purse, and told me to take it because she could always make some more. She said for me not to tell anybody, for it would get her into trouble.

"I have never forgot her for doing that kind thing for me, and if I could, I would take her out of that place and see that she got a good place to stay and a nice husband to take care of her. Her kind heart showed me that her understanding overruled the average moral conception of society against prostitutes."

## DRINKING—MAKING YOUR OWN BREW

"Do you belong to any organizations?" I asked, and he thought awhile. "Well, no. But come to think of it, I do kind of belong to one. There aren't any dues or nothing. It's the Brotherhood of Drinkers."

Most drifters seem to drink at one time or another, although most of them haven't what we'd call a "drinking problem." "Drinking problem? Me? Why sure. I don't get enough of it."

Commercialism has taken over all phases of the liquor industry but not entirely so for all serious drinkers. These aren't the upper-middle-class practitioners of the "Wine Art," excellent though home-made wines turn out to be.

Making your own brew appeals to the Cougar's ingenuity and his sense of being able to make do with what he can get most easily. Take a cake of yeast, two gallons of water, and cut a potato into small squares. The potato will activate the yeast. Then add any kind of fruit, fresh or dried. If the fruit is dried, add one cup of it for two gallons of water. Six fresh oranges will do if you haven't got orange juice and want to go that route. Seventy-two hours is the magic time. It'll get sour if left much longer—it'll turn to vinegar. You just learn to taste test: when it burns your throat, it's ready.

And all over America and throughout Cougar land, you see the fellows creating their own home-made brew. One Cougar in the bottoms along the Little Wabash in southern Illinois would leave the spouts of his bottles open above the ground. It was with a sense of pride and accomplishment that he showed me his family farm operation. It occurred to me that in the past, on the edges of jungles, I had seen these booze burying grounds, unaware of the creativity that was involved. I've seen the approving glances of misunderstanding matrons in grocery lines, where a tippler would be exchanging food stamps for dried prunes and raisins. All you need to do is get some water and set up your batch. Now if you save some of the stuff in the bottom and add a gallon of water you can reduce the setting-up time to maybe forty-eight hours.

In jails, in camps, in the broad reaches of America, this is the way of the times, as it was yesteryear. It's so easy, so reliable in effect—figjack, prunejack, pineapplejack. Just take a tall can of pineapple juice, and one-half the amount of water, and about a quarter pound of sugar and perhaps a quarter cube of yeast. You'd better start tasting after forty-eight hours, if you can wait that long. Making your own stash is creative and cheap and individual.

Making their own judgments and tending to be insensitive or unaware of the opinions of others, some Cougars are given to developing drinking problems of greater intensity than they recognize or admit. They like to think of being drunk as the alternative to not drinking, and they generally are outraged when blood tests show that they have more alcohol than the limits permissible by local police authorities.

I knew a woman Cougar who had cooked in lumber camps and followed the harvests for many years. After her two children went out on their own, she took to drinking. From time to time she would wind up in jail for disorderly conduct. She wasn't what I would call a drunk; rather, she felt it was her own right to sing and shout and socialize and wake up and bring alive people who looked down in the mouth on life. Whose peace was she disturbing? Not those with her in the bars surely, and not those walking down the streets. She was largely celebrating, and most people around her would get to smiling and even laughing.

She depended upon the public defender. She didn't have any lawyer. She vaguely felt she was counteracting the loss of individuality among people and the ways we are all manipulated into endless conformities by more governmental requirements.

For her, drinking helped her to be herself, or so she thought. And she would say, "The bottle helps us see others as they are. I raised my children right enough, worked hard, and I'm not ashamed to let myself be seen as I am. Nothing to hide. And besides, you wouldn't believe it, but I'm a shy person underneath it all. You know, I'm also an old-time gal and all of us, men and women, were hard drinkers. Usually could hold our liquor, too."

One aging Cougar said, "Drinking? Let me show you something," and he took a card out of his billfold and read,

" 'Wee get too soon old und too late schmart!' It's in many-colored glass down in Hoffman's bar in San Jose. I look in there when I'm passing through."

# Cougarish Social Attitudes

If God came to earth, he certainly wouldn't believe in God.

All you get on welfare is a room and some food stamps. If they're going to buy me, they're not going to buy me that cheap.

I don't want to do anything to anybody. If the world falls off its axis let it fall.

I would rather have my own way than do what people

say is the proper thing to do.

Conversations with Cougars

The Cougar type displays many of the values associ-
ated with the West when it was young. He is impulsive and
adventurous; formulator of his own plans, follower of his
own decisions; given to a tough exterior but with a gentle,
even sentimental, heart; ready to fight for principle but not
for the sake of fighting; willing to submit as long as he
maintains his own inner integrity. Interpersonally, Cougars
often display a lack of understanding of other humans.
They aren't able to put themselves in another's skin.

I also find that many of the Cougars' social values have
much in common with the lower working classes and the
upper upper classes but very little with the large middle
groups. Traditionally, the working classes have placed high
value on working with one's hands and back and have dis-
trusted those who have gained their knowledge largely from
books and who make their living through manipulation or
direction of others. Thus, "the experts"—the intellectuals
and the professionals, such as social workers, psychologists,
and doctors—are not to be trusted. Cougars have a feeling
of equality, of being as good as anyone else, and they expect
democratic reciprocity in human relationships.

Generally speaking, this proud self-assertiveness
among Cougars, which is also found among those with
inherited wealth in the highest social classes, is accom-
panied by an obliviousness to the ways institutions shape
human lives. Like the upper upper classes, Cougars do not
blame institutions for dominating their lives, though they
may have slightly different reasons for their feelings.

Because Cougars regard people as essentially equal,
they can relate easily to the very rich and independent

people they meet. They are likely to work a few weeks on their ranches or estates. Not being a social radical, the Cougar feels no resentment towards the rich or powerful, and in fact they may hit it off quite well. Rather, he tends to feel sorry for those shackled by numerous responsibilities, commitments, and possessions. He has a strong urge to get away to a simpler environment. Many a Cougar has later referred to one of these rich contacts as actually being just like himself underneath it all.

As the economic patterns and functions in society have changed—with men replaced by machines, and muscle power and ingenuity by technology and patterned programming—Cougars find the environment more and more confusing, if not downright irrational and hostile. However, instead of trying to strike back at society, they prefer to stand apart and drift about, trying to keep alive a past which they sometimes hardly knew. Western magazines, movies and dress appeal to them.

## UNIONIZATION

Unions and social welfare, established to cope with the problems of modern society, have not been congenial to most Cougars, who feel that such programs have been created by "them" and, of course, only restrict freedom of thought and movement. Most institutions are devoted to adapting people to fit into institutions. Standing in lines, filling out forms, and complying with bureaucratic procedures waste time and kill the spirit.

During the 1960s I had many spirited discussions with migrant workers. In particular, I talked with an aging Cougar who lived from time to time in the jungles along the American River and later moved into the catacombs along

Second, Third, and Fourth streets in Sacramento. In the summer he still picked fruit and in the winter did a little pruning.

Knowing that he was approaching the time when he wouldn't have the strength for physical work, that his sense of fairness and justice was well developed, and that he got along easily with strangers, I thought he might be very helpful in improving the lives of farm laborers.

One evening, with some hesitancy and high hopes, I told my friend that I had access to funds and would be able to pay his basic living costs (up to $200 a month) for a while if he would go to various labor camps in the central valleys and talk with workers, farmers, and labor contractors.

He could point out to them how everyone in agriculture could benefit by closer cooperation, possibly unionization, and by a united effort to educate people around our country as to the basic costs of producing and distributing food. In recent years the farm owner and the farm laborer hadn't got as much economic reward as other segments of the population. The abandonment of millions of farms was testimony to that. My Cougar friend had helped me develop this theme, so I was hardly ready for his response.

He rejected my proposal. He had thought that I had a higher regard for him. Now it appeared to him that I wanted to use him for my own ends, wanted him to change his style of life and mess around with other people's affairs.

We walked out of the bar onto Second Street, which was already being wrecked by urban renewal, though a few workingmen's hotels were open. I still hoped that he might change his mind. But under a corner light, I saw the hurt look in his eyes, and he said, "Lloyd, I know you mean well." And he offered me his hand in farewell. I never saw him again.

Another Cougar puts his feelings about unions like this: "A few years ago in the field, they got this union started and it's a little bit different; it really is. See, the Mexican people—I've worked with 'em a great deal and a lot of 'em's talked to me, and they talk straight. A lot of them don't like the union because it hinders them. They can only do certain jobs—certain specified jobs the union tells them to do. They just can't go out and do what they want to do at random. That's all. And it ties them down, and they have to pay penalties. Like one Mexican woman told the group I was in. She talked in English and said she had missed two days work, so the union, the Chavez union—I shouldn't use his name I suppose—fired her. In order to get that book back again so she could work in the field she had to pay $10.50. Well, she has to live, she has to work, so she had to go back and pay another $10.50 to get her book renewed, with a scolding, 'Don't miss no more days.' Well, I don't think the union should do the firing. I should think the foreman of the company should. Well, I'm not for it, and I'm not against the union. I shut my mouth on things I don't understand. That's the best way. And if it's not for me I glide off into other work. I have a good many capacities. I'm kind of jack-of-all-trades but I'm master of not one of them."

WELFARE

"Welfare programs are the enemy of humankind," seems to be the prevalent Cougar attitude. Many a Cougar has pointed out that his own marriage floundered in part through his wife's preferring to stick with the dependable welfare check rather than risk with him the uncertainties of employment and living in general.

One friend wrote me a letter describing his feelings about welfare.

"The brasseros [Mexican farm workers] worked hard for there money so they want them back. But there is people hear that will work for it if they pay the write price and they will beet the brasseros or, as was proved, do better. I know on a job last year we beet them every day we worked. But if you will give them more wellfare they are not going to work.

"There is three thousand men here in Stockton drawing checkes that could put out the work for all of the men that they bring in. That is why you can't get help here. If they would pay a good wage and stop your wellfere for those that don't need it, you would have plenty of help. But if you will pay a man & family $300 wellfair and he can only make $220 to $300 working, what would you do? There is a lot of them here.

"About three contractors bring more busses down there than they need so that they can say that they are two or three thousand men short. Then the employment office turns that in. It goes to the state, then they ask for help and they don't realy need it.

"If you have five or six children and don't know a traid, you can make more on the state than you can working."

## RELIGION

"I believe in religion as a way of life, not as a religion," one fellow told me.

Organized religion can hardly be said to be a new institution in the West. Most every frontier community eventually had its own church, with circuit-riding ministers arriving at least once a week. Before long there would be three churches, two for Protestants and one for Catholics.

At one time or another, most Cougars have attended church. However, few survived the habit beyond a few months. It's not that they didn't believe in much that they heard or didn't accept the idea that there might be a God or a unifying force in the universe, but they found the Bible stories dull and the Sunday school teachers and ministers even duller. What could the implausible biblical stories have to do with their own lives or the lives of the people they knew? They see people in their Sunday dress and manner who during the week do not live lives of generosity, understanding, or forgiveness. The pillars of the church often have a clay footing.

The Cougar counts himself out of the religious process, all the while stoutly defending anyone's right to his beliefs or lack thereof. Going to church is not something he condemns; it is just not "his thing."

"Jesus was a tramp," one Cougar pointed out. And he went on to relate his own shattering experience. "The first god-damned time I made up my mind to be religious, I went in this here mission. It was warm, the music got to me, and there seemed to be a nice spirit, and I got to thinking, maybe this isn't such a shirk organization after all. Then you know what happened? A bum—I'd seem him down in the park earlier—comes up to me with a basket for me to put some money in. Can you imagine that? They were putting the bum on me!"

## WAR AND THE SERVICE

(I wrote this in 1961 while I was in Pennsylvania. Due to my southern accent I was referred to as "The Rebel," which gave me the inspiration to write this song.)

Back in 1861 the Civil war was on.
It was brother against brother,
Father against son. The Yankee
wore the blue coat, the Rebel wore
the gray, both sides lost, each and
every day. Their hearts were filled
with sorrow, that men in war will
know, hoping that tomorrow, back
home they would go. Said Mr. Lincoln, so
great and tall, together we stand, but divided we
fall, this tragic war, would never have been, if
people could realize, that men are men, regardless
of race, color, or creed, if we all work together, we
will succeed. Even today one hundred years later
the price of freedom is high in order for men to
stay free then other men must die.

Wm. R. Evans ("Hobo Bill")
Plumsteadville, Pennsylvania, 1961

Many Cougars joined the armed forces and sought out action assignments. Sir Hugh Boustead is a classic example of an individual with this Cougar trait. In his teens he deserted one branch of the service to get into another where there was more action. Through the influence of his family, he was able to succeed. Although Boustead lives a life of independent accomplishment, he probably never quite understands those around him or even himself.

World War II was a major factor in the lives of many Cougars. There was a great demand for the young and able-bodied. Jobs were plentiful, and future Cougars left their homes to find employment in shipyards and elsewhere, frequently living with a runaway girl or marrying some allotment-conscious girl. Often they managed to enter military service a year before they were officially old enough. They saw from three to six years of military service, and many earned military honors in various phases of combat duty. Upon leaving the service, often as heroes, they found their marriages already shattered or uninteresting. They were unable to assume a stable role in the economic system—not that many of them were looking for stability.

A great many were injured during military service. In a surprising number of instances, they played down their physical disabilities to avoid going in the hospital and, instead, get an earlier release. Thus, their physical disabilities often remained untreated until later in life. When they realized they could go to a military hospital, they often were reluctant to do so, not caring for the bureaucracy, the red tape, and the selling out they imagined necessary to be a "good patient."

One Cougar put it this way: "The psychiatrist who has to talk to you when you get out of the service asked me this question I'll never forget. 'What would you do if you were in the middle of the desert and you saw a battleship?' I thought I'd misunderstood him and had to ask him to repeat. I said I'd probably do the same thing as you would if you were in the middle of the desert and saw a Cadillac. He didn't ask me any more questions after that. He knew I was OK. . . . I wasn't going to play with those puzzles. It was childish. I had the confidence. But I didn't want to play with blocks. I wanted my discharge. . . . When you're in the service you're like a celebrity. When you get out, you're just another chump. Like you were never there. Medals, citations. Never used the GI bill. Didn't want it or need it."

While in the service Cougars invariably found themselves in conflict with "the system." The brig and the guardhouse were familiar stopovers. They just could not see how staying in town an extra couple hours at night would make any difference to winning the war or the peace.

## LAW AND ORDER

Cougars simply don't observe laws that don't seem to make any sense to them, such as stopping for traffic at stop signs when there isn't another car in sight.

Mel Settle wrote me: "I have hawked the car now for room rent and don't know how I'm going to get it out. But I couldn't sleep in it with her, although she was willing. She never complained one time. But if they catch you in this country they will pick you up, that is a man and a woman in a car sleeping. I don't know why, but they think something is wrong."

By this code, however, they do not pretend to be innocent when they're not. If they are arrested and they feel they've broken the law—even though they regard the law as foolish—they do not plead innocent. As one Cougar put it, "I was guilty and I took my punishment like a man." He described how he and a friend met after work to have a few beers. This was in Stockton, and they talked about their families in Sacramento some fifty miles away. In the process they made a small wager as to who could get home to Sacramento first. They ran out of the bar, and one fellow sped away in his car. The other Cougar awoke to the fact that his auto was at home—fifty miles away. The race idea seemed like fun, and not to be bested, he looked in the cars along the street, and sure enough, one had a key.

And off he went, barreling up Highway 99 faster than the legal speed limit. He tried to pass a car, but as he was halfway around it, he could see an oncoming car bearing

down on him. He swerved off the road onto the left shoulder
and into the ditch. When the highway patrol reached him,
they quickly determined that he had been drinking and also
that he was in a stolen car. He was sentenced to six months
in prison. With a skillful lawyer he could have gotten off.
But no, as he pointed out to me, he was guilty and had to
pay the penalty.

It is in such situations as this that Cougars land in jail.
Fighting when drunk and disturbing the peace are common
raps.

One fellow told me that he had got to thinking about
the copper-wire shortage and wanted to do something to
help. So he climbed an abandoned telephone pole, with
several people looking on, and started to cut down some
wire. When apprehended, he refused to get a lawyer to try
to get the charges lowered. Incidentally, this Cougar
thought very highly of the public-utility companies; he had
worked briefly for one of them. He was just beered up and
"trying to be helpful." In jail he felt like a fool, but he
wasn't about to compromise his integrity when it came to
the enforcement of the law.

If a fellow pleads guilty, he is sent to jail and he can get
it all over with. But if he stalls and fights back legally,
there's the uncertainty and also the likelihood of paying a
lawyer who may not be as ethical as his cell mates. And
when the lawyer is able to work out a compromise with the
D.A. or judge, the Cougar assumes that someone has been
bought off, either with money or through influence.

Cheating, lying, not "taking your medicine," manipu-
lating the courts, buying off lawyers, and using community
pressure are not for a Cougar. He refuses to stoop so low as
to use any of the accepted ways of tampering with justice.

# Authority, the Enemy

If he acted too high above me, I'd walk off.

Authority is a 'yes' or 'no' thing. Puts one on the level of a young child.

I'm like a wild stallion in a corral. He doesn't think it's proper for somebody to throw a rope around him to hold him in restraint, or lead him around.

People tell me I shouldn't smoke for I'll get cancer. But I smoke because if I didn't smoke, I probably would get an ulcer which is a cousin to a cancer. I could get a cold right here in this room as well as by walking in the rain.

There's a right way and there's the best way.

I myself understand and side with an individual who's unwilling to buckle down to an authority figure; specifically when the person holding the authoritative position abuses that position and uses it for personal gain at the cost of damaged feelings, physical injury, and mental anguish of those he's over.

Observations by Cougars

The person who accepts freedom as an inalienable human right is bound to have a lifetime of set-tos with those who impose restraints. As a rule, the process of growing up, with its cuffs and blows, settles an individual down into reasonable conformity. And generally, most people make their peace with law and order and the established ways of society. To some extent even Cougars do, but not without deep personal pain.

There is a fine distinction between a Cougar's attitude toward law and his attitude toward authority. One fellow told me: "I have respect for the law as the highway patrol and the police. They have a job to do and do it. . . . Yes, I resent authority but respect the law."

In considering the early lives of Cougars, we have seen their pattern of dropping out of school and getting off on their own. Many times I've heard the refrain, "School didn't fit me." More often than not their childhood was happy. Parents tended to be loving and understanding.

Some Cougars had an upbringing along the lines of the American Indian child: little criticism, very little guidance, and much warm acceptance.

Because the teenage Cougar went off on his own at an early age, he didn't experience the buffetings most teenagers undergo. He resisted being forced to conform or give in and yield to working together with others. So he went into adulthood having missed out on the experience common to most of us, that of being molded by our social environments, especially by our school life.

Viewed in this light, is it any wonder that the adult Cougar is unwilling to toe the mark as fashions, styles, folkways, and popular opinions would dictate?

As one fellow put it to me, "People are very hard to understand. They accuse you of what you're not actually doing. They see you go into a bar and think you're getting drunk. My gosh, you gotta go in sometimes to get out of the cold and keep warm, or to get a pack of cigarettes, to see someone, or to relieve yourself. I don't know why people get so fixed in their thoughts."

Another fellow said, "It's the 'don't' part that irritates me. I'm not a child anymore. I have restraint enough when I'm told to do something for the sake of the job, but that's different from someone trying to tell me what to do in his way of doing it. Can't a fellow be told what to do and left to do it in his own way?"

"If you don't offer strong suggestions, how are you going to get someone to change," I asked one Cougar. He thought a bit and said, "A number of ways. Maybe, say to him 'Don't you think you ought to,' or again make the suggestion but let him make his own decision. Yeah, 'How do you think we can solve this problem?' or 'What kind of a plan do you have, what do you most want to do?'"

"Authority is not the man," Kenneth Hunt told me.
"It's the way man can use his authority which makes the
two come out totally different. Authority is law, or basic
rules and regulations. Where a man is the administrator of
authority, it is misuse by the administrator which is often
taken as abuse. For example, teachers, employers, law-
enforcement officials should never demand in an authoritative manner that a person do his command, for this not only
can, but possibly will, damage the commandment as well as
the person being commanded. If a person is asked to do
something without any overtones of visible authority, he will
likely show respect for being asked to do something—
respect for being respected. In other words, if you want to
throw rocks, then we'll both throw them; but if it's cotton
you choose, then it's OK."

Another Cougar, Ken Smedley, who had become foreman of an auto-wrecking yard, tried to explain how he
could both be a boss and yet not bossy. "There's just one
way to treat people. Think of them as people. I don't boss
anyone around. I say, 'I need this, will you take it off for
me?' I'll ask and not *tell*. Nothing to it. It's the only way to
do it."

The following personal log gives a rare peek into the
conflicts of a middle-aged Cougar who was pressured into
becoming a ship's officer.

## FLOYD SOULE

With quick, efficient movements, he has been almost too
restless to stay at sea. He's built his own ship and remodeled
houses. From shirt to sock line, he's covered with tatoos by
artists in many ports of the world.

## LOG OF THE S.S. F. T. SOULE

*January 13, 1967:* As the result of well-intentioned urgings from former officers, captains and port captains, friends and neighbors, I take the plunge.

*September 1:* Back to school again after thirty years and rough sledding. Interesting subject matter although heart not really in it.

*November 6:* Start sitting for my license. Things are so-so.

*November 16:* Down but not out. Failed on 'Rules of the Road.'

*November 18:* Shipped out S.S *Pioneer Contractor* (thirty day voyage—London-bound).

*December 18:* Begin sitting anew.

*January 5:* The goal achieved. The long awaited document, #344999.

*January 10:* In New York for U.S.L. [United States Lines] assignment. Retire from the N.M.U. after thirty years!

*January 13:* Join the M. M. [Merchant Marine] at $1000.

*January 13:* Assigned to the S.S. *American Rover* as third officer (deck).

*January 13-14-15:* On Board, meditating, wondering, alone and skeptical (of it all).

*January 15:*    At Chester Shipyard. Self-confined to dry-dock over the weekend. Night mate offers to delve into the mysteries of Loran for me. Six hours on Saturday and again a like amount on Sunday. With the light slowly beginning to dawn.

*January 16:*    Still in drydock. Taken in hand by the regular third and second mates, who are twenty-two years and twenty-three years, respectively, for a cook's tour of the vessel, explaining how the hatch and winches operate. More Loran [a long-range navigational system] instruction. Begin on Decca [another navigational system]. Really a fascination, but still as much a mystery as ever. Chief officer has telephoned the Master in New York that he really has a greenhorn aboard. I am immediately transferred to the eight to twelve watch, from the twelve to four. Fortunately no hard feelings. Spent the evening aboard teaching the night mate RADAR plotting problems. Also learn about Reflection Radar Plotting, i.e., directly on the scope! Fascinating!

*January 17:*    A dull, dreary, boring day eight to five. Roamed aimlessly about the ship. Tried to help correct charts. Not too successful. Difficulty in making myself useful.

*January 17:*    On watch for the first time at 8:00 P.M. Sorry. 20:00. Ship at anchor when I take over, Delaware River. What follows a never-to-be-forgotten nightmare! *ORDERS!*
    "Heave up the anchor, Put out anchor lights, Put out deck lights! Put on the running lights! Half speed Ahead. Log all times of speed changes!" Then the KILLER!

WHAT IS THE TIME OF EBB TIDE AT THE C. & D.
[Chesapeake & Delaware] CANAL!

ZOOM! Suddenly we are in the canal, and I am supposed to log the name, number, and the time each aid to
navigation passed! The bridges I get. However, half way
through I miss a light and when the Captain asks me our
position I ruefully tell him that I am lost, I don't know.
Fortunately there is a PILOT aboard. For the first time in
thirty years at sea I can smoke legally on the bridge. I light
up a cigar, but it is flat and tasteless and I soon give it up. I
am alternately hungry and thirsty. TOUGH! My kidneys
are bursting but I manage to hang on. I have to ! From 8:00
P.M. until midnight is an eternity. Spend from midnight
until 1:00 A.M. writing up my first log. Afraid of missing an
entry and equally afraid of putting in too much. Not many
visible entries but all must be painfully and painstakingly
hand printed. I am exhausted and beat!

*January 18:*  Arrive at Baltimore for docking. I am aft
again. Malfunctioning walkie-talkie or malfunctioning
"me," a combination of both. I press the wrong button at
the wrong time, and the air is blue with megaphoned orders
from the bridge by the Chief Mate! I fail to repeat orders
exactly as spoken. At long last we are tied up, and I am exhausted and wringing wet although it is 20 degrees. Tied up
by 9:30 A.M. without tugs due to strike and again I have
mike fright. Somehow the day passes. I neglect to log the
time of the longshoremen's arrivals and departures and
catch proper hell! Forget to close the main fire line drains
aft and as a result the after gang gets a proper soaking, at
25 degrees! All most unhappy. Undocking fairly smooth
although I am beat, tired, and alone. On watch shortly
afterwards eight to twelve. Little sleep tonight as we arrive

and dock at Philadelphia at 3:00 A.M. tomorrow.

*January 20:*   Arrive New York 9:00 A.M. If it weren't for $1000 I.O.U. in M. M. & P., would throw in the towel. May anyway. Spend the day checking cargo. Buying useless expensive uniforms, hat, shoulder boards, etc. $80 in all. Big money my foot. Don't even get to feel the warmth of it.

*January 21:*   Saturday. So what! Spend eight hours walking from one end of the ship to the other, unable to smoke, setting an example to longshoremen. Who couldn't care less. They break into cargo at will, and I am helpless to do anything about it. Great temptation to get stoned tonight but won't. Dread tomorrow's first watch at sea alone.

*January 23:*   On watch tonight. Darker than the proverbial witch's. . . . At 7:50 a sneaky fisherman refuses to give way and I watch Tom (second mate, twenty-three) calmly observe and plot his C.P.A. [course port ahead], which is '0'. In the end the other fellow chickens out and all's well. All well with me until 11:00. At 8.5 miles I pick up a target 4 points on the port bow. Plot and discover his C.P.A. is '0'. I continue to watch him. Of course if he has no RADAR he can't see me as the visibility is limited. At 3.6 miles he shows up visually, still with a C.P.A. of '0'. He's not going to chicken out even if he is in the wrong. I must hold my course and speed, *until* EXTREMIS sets in. This is a point where a collision is inevitable, and I now must change course to avoid this situation. At 2 miles still bearing down. A monstrous 300-foot white Russian Trawler at 15 knots aimed right for my midships. At 1½ miles I make the choice: 40 degrees right helm which must have thrown everyone out of bed. The trawler is still homing on me, lit up like a Christmas tree, and I can see dozens of fisherman on deck watching the spectacle. Only when we were 1¼ mile apart did he deign to alter his course to the reverse direction, wagging his tail at me as he turned and ran! The quartermaster was shaking as was I. Obviously a time to call for the captain, but the action happened so fast that I didn't. END of WATCH!

*January 24:* More expected admonitions today. Don't enter calm seas or clear visibility ever in the log book. Apparently the less said, the better. The tendency to copy whatever the fellow wrote before you must be curbed, tho difficult, as there is really so little to say. Everything apparently written with the idea foremost in mind that some day whatever was written might appear in a court of law where such namby-pamby writings will be torn to shreds by searching, shrewd, maritime lawyers. Morning watch passes after a fashion. Trying to send in weather reports and learn to make weather maps simultaneously. Thank Heavens there is no sun. My celestial navigation will be most painful.

*January 25:* I have maintained all my life that when I ask someone a simple, civil, and intelligent question, I expect to be answered in like fashion. From the Master I don't get an answer of any sort to any question, and from the mate usually a string of oaths.

*January 26:* After the smoothness of last night's watch had expected this morning's to be the same. What a dreamer! Smoke alarm shorted out, and I had the mate in a tizzy trying to remedy the buzzing and flashing lights. Had to rewrite yesterday's log due to my type of definition and descriptions. It does not *drizzle* on the ocean. And a lesson in protocol. I have finally not said please and thank you to my watch standers for two days. Instead: VERY WELL! How ridiculous can you get! Inadvertently I said it to the Master today and really received my come-uppance for it. Informed that one does not address one's superior as 'very well' but rather as 'yes sir' and that they in turn will address me as 'very well,' as I am the lowest ranking officer in the ship! A dubious honor! Part of the hazing that goes along with this job? I can well do without it, thank you . . . sir!

After my watch is over at noon, I write up the smooth log and to *try* to avoid errors. I take a hell of a lot of time. So much that I never get into the mess room before 12:20. The Master directed me today to be there not later than 12:15 or not to enter at all! Such a temptation to tell him off orally, but I forebore the temptation. His snide attempts at "spirit-crushing" are all too apparent.

I look fondly at the shelf of unread books before me this trip and am sad. And at the stack of unanswered letters and unmailed Xmas Cards and am even sadder. Is it worth it? What have I gained? Better yet, what have I lost?

*January 26:*   (midnight) Another watch over. Uneventful. No ships. No criticism of my log for a change. Master up once for minutes. No good evening or nothin'. So pitch him!

*January 27:*   P.M. watch. Uneventful save for dropping my tea pot and making a terrific clatter. After a prolonged coughing session put on by the old man, I have decided that cigar smoking has been indefinitely banned from the bridge. Tough on White Owl stockholders. One interesting development happened tonight. The chief engineer in the engine room decided to make a switch from bridge control to engine and pushed the necessary knobs or buttons down below. As he did a terrific buzzing sound emanated from the bridge console, which try as I might I was unable to stop. In desperation I called the engine room for a remedy. They merely suggested pushing all the buttons at my disposal once more. I did. The only thing that happened was that the old man came flying up onto the bridge with fire in his eyes, turned a wheel which I hadn't seen in the dark and all was serene once more . . . save for my stomach! It was Gone with the Breeze.

*January 28:* P.M. watch. This "was" the watch that "was." At 8:00 P.M. with trembling knees I clumb the mile long flight of steps to the bridge. There on the scope were no less than eighteen targets, half of them neatly plotted for me to carry on from, with the "rots of ruck" greeting from Gene, who then promptly disappeared. Nothing crucial for the next few minutes. Then I suddenly remembered that I was supposed to get a Decca Fix every half hour *and* if the current set was to southward I was to make equal compensation to the Northward on the GYRO. Already we had a 7 degree allowance, 3 degrees for GYRO error, 2 degrees for set and 2 for leeway! So I had to remember what to add and what to subtract from. In my shuttling between the chart room and the RADAR scope, I practically dismembered the chief officer who when I needed him most was there to help me. So under his guidance and tutelege, the watch passed. Saw on the scope nearly 150 ships in all, plotted over half of them, often 10 to 12 at one time. Then the constant switching from the six to the sixteen mile range kept me busy as the former plots had to be erased while the new ones were established. As a result I never after 8:30,

sorry 20:30, ever did set foot into the chart room again. I
*might* have gotten by alone without mishap, but I'd have
been packed and ready for a restraining jacket if Mr. Shiff-
man hadn't provided. . . .

*January 29:*    A.M.–P.M. watch. Through the Straits of
Dover and up the Coast of Holland. Buoys to the right and
left, lightships everywhere and ships by the score. I spent
the morning plotting without a smoke, a drink of water or
an extra breath. Interesting and no little tiring. Picked up
pilot at twelve noon and I'm off until 3:00 P.M. docking.
Not too bad, for a change. Only forgot three "yes sirs" and
one repeat of orders. And missed the name of one tug.
Through at 4:00 P.M. and on watch again at 8:00 P.M.
until midnight, learning. Then on again until noon today.
Sixteen hours straight and am too tired to sleep, and going
ashore out of the question. Dozed on and off this afternoon.
Sailing at 3:00 A.M. tomorrow the 31st. What a life!

*February 9:*    My utopian way of life seems to be swiftly dis-
integrating in front of my eyes, even now as I write. The 101
initial arguments which I presented and digested to my
alter ego outward bound were so insignificant when com-
pared to the mental fatigue and depression which I am now
trying to cope with and seem unable to overcome. On many
ships I've known officers off watch relieve their boredom by
belting down Scotch or a reasonable facsimile as though it
were going out of production, and this ship is no different.
Possibly for the lack of companionship and the boredom in
a job, this is increasingly growing as more and more automation and faster turn-arounds become the order of the
day. An unhealthy situation to my way of thinking.
    What then is the ultimate solution to the present situ-

ation? A collection of moronic idiots to man these vessels; the same as found on some ships today who take the "couldn't care less" attitude, and who would apply paint with a pitchfork if ordered to do so? Or a collection of greedy men, or six crews for five ships, or a ninety day on, ninety day off routine, or even better yet, radio-controlled and operated ships?

Passed Bishop's Rock this morning on my watch but somehow or other I managed to miss the damned thing entirely!

*February 13:*   Off Cape Race and only slightly more than twenty-four hours left before reaching Boston. Temperature at zero or below. Have a lookout posted around the clock on the windward side of the bridge naturally! This morning, with the visibility down to zero, in the midst of squally blinding snow and with nothing on the RADAR for twenty miles, I brought the lookout inside the wheelhouse. After all, with his back braced against the wind which blew in forty to fifty m.p.h. gusts, there was little that he could see outside anyhow. I'd seen this procedure adopted on many ships before so that I felt that I was only acting humanely and within my rights as a watch officer. However the old man's frown soon convinced me that I was wrong once again, as he quoted the Coast Guard Rules verbatim and so out again the lookout was quickly sent!

*February 16:*   Off pier #62 at 7:00 A.M. for an eight o'clock arrival. The longshoremen stream aboard and the watch officers, save for myself, are equally as agile in descending the gangway. Although there are cargo mates aboard by night, I spend the next two days "watching cargo" as well as watching the petty and not-so-petty thievery so rampant on the New York waterfront. The "high-pressure" hat and my insignificant rank fail to deter them in the least iota, and some of their useless pilferings really fill me with disgust. The presence of a watchman and a ship's officer are meaningless insofar as they are concerned, and although I hear nothing but complaints relative to containerized cargo and mutterings of grim forbodings in the future, I for one am glad that hopefully they have at last met their match.

*February 17:*   Paid off and homeward bound on the first plane available. Bitter and still unreconciled to my recent rude awakening that "all is not gold that shines."

## CONCLUSION

Aside from the aesthetics of it all:

1.   Discovering that the multiple pressures are terrific.
2.   That what appeared to be a simple problem in a classroom or at home now appears to be a nightmare of responsibility.
3.   So many unforseen obstacles have arisen to obstruct my peace and happiness.
4.   Possibly the grass isn't really greener after all, and that uneasy lies the head that wears the officer's cap.
5.   The pressures of trying to follow through with half a dozen simultaneous commands as evidence by my first watch through the C & D Canal. True, I managed to keep water under the keel, but just barely!

My rationaliziation from my present predicament:

1.   The younger officers, barely in their twenties, have yet to learn the meaning of either caution or fear, or so it would seem. After four years of schoolship training, thence straight to a ship so that electronic gear and high-speed ships are second nature to them.

2.   Those my age or older have grown up with the situation gradually, through the passing years, Loran, Radar, Decca, so that the assimilation was a gradual one.

3.   ME! YESTERDAY! BOOM! Here today. Understand it all or perish!

4.   It's somewhat difficult to change my way of life, and I'm not sure I want to.

5.   I find myself resenting the loss of hard-won, proven, and fought-for freedoms when finding now that of necessity I must become a conformist, lest I dent the company's image.

6.   I discover the officer's union, the M. M. & P., to be tainted with corruption, underhandedness, job-selling, and more.

7.   I find myself still saddled with a double hardship, the pressures of the ever-continuing multiple-learning process.

8.   So shall I swallow my pride and become a conformist?

9.   What have I gained and what have I proven?

10.   In becoming a conformist I face the loss of individuality, to be swallowed up in a morass of nameless faces.

11.   Already frustration looms high on the horizon.

12.   The Chief Officer, my immediate superior, no doubt an excellent seaman, posting a fourth (sixteen years) issue of Master's Certificate, sweating out the day when he will have his own ship, which day may never arrive, which

makes him grumpy, disagreeable, snide, obnoxious and damned hard to get along with.

14.　Now the gains seem to be only of monetary value, rather than aesthetic.

15.　Possibly all of the above arguments are selfish ones.

## THE PROS AND CONS OF IT ALL

Reviewing the past thirty-odd years:

A.　When a license was desired, not available; when available, was not desired.

B.　As an a.b. [able-bodied seaman] the PROS:

1.　Have always enjoyed working with my hands.
2.　Freedom of speech.
3.　Freedom of changing jobs.
4.　Pursuit of individuality.
5.　Freedom of dress.
6.　Available camaraderie, to be accepted or rejected.
7.　Choice of watches, i.e., working hours.
8.　Availability of time off, especially overseas, scenery bum.
9.　Freedom to read, write, think and do as I saw fit.
10.　Now studying further will tend to become a monopoly.
11.　Loss of freedom to change ships, to revisit old friends, overseas.

C.　As an a.b. the CONS:

1.　Indeterminable wheel watches.

2.   Long, cold lookouts.
3.   Alcoholic, uncooperative, shirking shipmates.
4.   Aloft in all kinds of weather.
5.   Over the side likewise.

Thus I have proven a point, if this was then my intent; that I do possess the brains and ability or whatever it takes to study for, sit for, and receive a license. So what! Now what!

In the final analysis the decision must be mine. What will it be? Am I here in spite of myself or because of myself? I'm not worried about the responsibilities. But is it my duty to continue blindly on because of the faith that friends, family, neighbors, former shipmates, and officers have shown in me? Is my future theirs? It's like trying to rationalize an unrational situation.

Try as I may not to, I find myself approaching each coming watch with dread, almost akin to hatred, not with fear and trembling, but hopelessly confused with the myriad of duties to be remembered and the corrections which must continually be made in mistakes of previous watches.

Is it conscience or cowardice which causes me to think and write thusly?

Now you have a rough idea of my day-to-day ironies, frustrations and so-called sticky situations which inevitably arise. I find it difficult to be something that I'm really not, and the fact that everyone is on my side offers little consolation.

So while an idea has been fulfilled, the shock of reality has been quite an eye-opener.

# Scenery Buff and Animal Lover

I have a small creek that goes by that flows all year long. And it's fed by a spring so that's real fresh water, and I'll carry it, a bucket or two and have real *real* fresh spring water. That's rare to you city folks. You *fresh* city folks have got what man wants you to have. *water* Look what I got. I'll dig me a little catch hole and I'll have real good spring water, the best. And I've got real nice scenery, real scenery of hills and rollings.

Eric Furbish

I'd bring out a transistor radio and set it down on the wall. Three lizards would crawl over near it and cock

*my*
*pets*
their heads. They liked the music, and I'd turn it round and full as I could. That baby lizard was about an inch-and-a-half long and sure did like that music. They were my pets.

Kenneth Hunt

You may see a Cougar sitting on a ridge looking across at a burned-off hillside, black where the grass had been, gray where the day before there had been brushpiles, the green of the lower boughs of oaks singed brown. He may have helped in this burning-off when the cattle rancher needed him to help out for a few days to make sure the fires started didn't get away—fires burned under permit from regional fire authorities. There are those who see beauty in these black, gray-brown burned areas, and in their minds they picture the rebirth of grass and foliage.

Such a view isn't usually in guidebooks. It's entirely different with the jet-setter or Appalachian or Sierra Mountain clubber who all too often searches out the greenest valley, swiftest stream, rockiest pile of rocks, or bluest lake, spending an inordinate amount of the earth's and society's resources in so doing.

The Cougar sees what is around him. Maybe it's just a monarch butterfly drying its wings in preparation for the morning's takeoff sitting on a thistle, the white seeds floating away.

*hello,*
*beautiful*
"In the fall they have these large butterflies. They're deep orange with lots of black lines. They're so large they don't flutter their wings; they glide. And they seem to hang around the eucalyptus tree. I guess they get some food or some fungus off the leaves. But they're beautiful. Oh yes they are—they're beautiful. They glide; way up high they glide. You

can just sit there and watch them. And they circle and they glide. And do you know something? I didn't know this, but you know something, from out of me, it came out of me, I says 'Hello, beautiful,' just about that loud, 'Hello, beautiful.' It was really pretty to see 'em—I don't know what I say, just talking—a lot of people that hear me think I'm crazy. But anyway, I'm not. Cause I enjoy, I see them. I see what they do, and I see how they feel, and I feel what they're for and what they mean. I don't know how to say what I feel inside. And you know your voice, the voice brings them down to you. They came so low; they were two and three feet circling over my head and I'd just whisper, just as loud as this, 'Hi, beautiful, hi.'

"You know I guess I can hear like a dog's ear, very sensitive. But it did; it brings them down, believe it or not. And it seems like there are only certain ones around—maybe I've got pets out of them. I haven't seen them in the last two or three weeks. They've flown down below where they have that large butterfly festival every year. They're a very knowing butterfly. Maybe they didn't come down because of my voice, but anyway they came down and it made me feel pretty good. And the saws don't ever bother them, no.

"One morning it was real icy on the ground. I thought I'd hurt one. I turned some wood over to throw it down below so we could easily get to the splitter, and I turned it over and there was a butterfly, one of those big butterflies on the ground. I looked her over. She didn't seem hurt, so I picked it up on one of those long eucalyptus tree leaves. It was a dry leaf, and—it was cold—and I moved it over to a sun ray, or a spot of the sun. And I sat down and I kept watching it, and I kept working and watching it, and in about ten minutes it opened up its wings and in its wings there was dew drops of water and the sun was warming it and I just let it stay there, half-hour or better, and I watched it, always kept checking on it, to see if it would fly.

"But then all at once, about forty-five minutes or an hour, I seen one up there flying around. I knew the air was warm enough cause this butterfly of the same type *it's* was flying around, or there was something wrong *time* with it. The wings seemed to be in fine shape, and *to fly* the body, so I got that leaf and I picked it up. It walked on the leaf and stayed on the leaf. I held it way up high, high as I possibly could. And I says, 'Well, it's time to fly, come on beautiful, fly, it's time to fly, come on, come on.' And you know, it did. Hmmmm. What a feeling. Hmmm. What a feeling of closeness. What a feeling. Closeness. I guess that's the word for it. It went up to the top of that eucalyptus tree—and they grow tall you know—and lit on a leaf. I knew I hadn't hurt it. That was real fine. I can put it down in words, but I can't put it down in feeling. You got to have that same feeling I guess, or do it, and then I guess you'd have the feeling. It's like I guess repairing a bird's wing and it was patched all up and you done it, and you send it out to its freedom and it flew away. I guess that's about the same too. . . .

"Ever really look at a hummingbird? Really ever look at a hummingbird? A lot of people see a hummingbird, but they don't *see* the hummingbird, never walk *watch* around it. When it's sitting on a limb or eating *the* some of that sweet stuff they hang up in back- *colors* yards. Walk around him in a circle real slow. *change* Watch the colors change. Colors change in the feathers. There are millions of colors, and they all blend together as you keep moving. They go from dark to firey dark, to light red, to blue to green. Very beautiful. In the speed of light. They can really fly, fly fast. Quite a bird.

When you look at them, look at them. Just don't see the bird, look at the bird. That's what I mean by looking. Look at the bird. That'll give you a feeling. That'll give you a feeling down inside, seeing something that others don't take time out to see or even know how to see."

Eric Furbish

"I am going to get away from this goofy Southern California hog marathon and all the shysters and clip artists and people trying to outdo the other in every *that* manner, shape, and form. Even the police hand *beautiful* out traffic citations like pancakes, and their *stud* fines are unreasonable as hell. I want to get a job back up near my stallion for awhile, perhaps as a caretaker of some private ranch or summer home. My appaloosa is only appaloosa in bloodline. His dam was a golden palomino. My stallion has a blaze face, three white stockings, and silver mane and tail. His pet name is 'El Cid,' but his registered name will be 'Benat El Rih,' an Arab name meaning "Son of the Wind." Oh, how I miss that beautiful stud. I spent many a happy hour and day with him."

Roy L. Nichols

"I remember how cold and brisk it had been my first day, but if you ever been in the redwood country then you know what I mean by cold. It's a fresh cold, an honest-to-God healthy and fresh cold that you don't seem to notice any chill."

Kenneth Hunt

"I brought a cat up there. I like cats. Very few people do, but I do. Named her 'Boots.' She had white boots; the rest of her was black. Very wonderful cat. Now up there in the back country above Ramona, there's a lot of coyotes and owls. That's where I lost Kitty Boots. Them owls, according to the Indians, and I believe they were right.

"Later I had a big black and white tomcat. Biggest cat I ever seen. Called him 'King.' Never handle kittens. That way they grow big. As for King. Well, they say you can't make friends with a cat. That's right. The cat makes friends with you. He likes you, you're in. He don't like you, you're out. That's why they don't like cats—very independent animal. You have to have patience, perseverence, respect, and you gotta be very slow. They'll come to you as they grow.

"Once I had nine kittens. They were entertainment for hours at a time for me. I'd just sit in a big chair, hold my feet up, and put paper bags down, and I'd *a cat* never touch the bags or nothing. Never scare *and* 'em. Nothing. And they would get in a bag with a *nine* kitten on the other side. They'd play through that *kittens* bag. When the bag moved, they'd move, and that bag would scoot all over the floor. And then they'd roll around in the bag. And then one would jump, one would run to another and the other one would just jump straight up in the air, land on all fours, sideways, with tail all fluffed up like a halloween cat. And the other one would rare his ears back. It was something.

"Well, up there was a lot of polecats. I had named every one of my cats, and they knew their names. And when I said good morning to one he knew it. You say good morning to an animal. Try it sometime. You're going to be acknowledged. You are. The cat quickly moves its tail. A dog will wiggle all over. Try it. People don't take enough time to do it. Well, I ain't got time for people.

"One time I kept smelling this polecat underneath the log cabin. What happened was my cats made one hell of a good playmate with this polecat. Yeah, brought him *the* home and everything else. He had a little smell on *pole* him, but not bad. So one day I left the screen door *cat* open, and inside there eating out of one of the cat's pans was this little teeny polecat. Boy! What am I going to do. I'm going to get him out. I say, you guys got him in here now you guys get him out. And they paid no more attention to me than the man in the moon. Then the polecat would walk over to one of the cats that was lying down and he'd just strike his paw at him—wouldn't pay no real attention. The polecat would walk around. It thumped with its hind feet. Don't you think it couldn't get on the table. Sure did. Climbed up on the chair, and from the chair on the table. Nosed all around. It's a clean animal. Unless you disturb them. Then look out.

"Well, I didn't get into that cabin until dark. Tried to get all the food outside. Every time a cat came out I wouldn't let it back in. Pretty soon the polecat was alone. He seen all the cats outside and out he wanted to go. And was I glad. Yep. No stink, no smell, very fine. That polecat stayed around there all the time. Never bothered me."

Eric Furbish

As boys, most Cougars like to hunt, but they give it up as they grow older. They are more likely to remember the look in the eyes of the last buck they shot than anything else. Their comment usually is "never again." The only instances I've known of older Cougars hunting were when they or someone they knew actually needed meat. Killing a deer isn't fair play or even play at all for that matter. How would you like to have an arrow or bullet in you?

"Yes, I believe Jarman is the last living horse to see active duty during World War II. At one time he was losing so much weight they were thinking it would be kinder to destroy him. But I took him to a veterinarian who filed his teeth so he could chew easier and I started hand feeding him a special diet. Now he's in good shape. He's just crazy about watching people. Smart too. The only horse I've heard of which figured out how to open the Portuguese gate—you know, where a stick is wired to another and you have to push the loop up. Yes, and he'll show you exactly where he wants his back scratched. I think his only disappointment in life is no one has asked him into their house."

*Old Jarman*

Conversation in 1973 with Charles B. Maddock

I've also noticed that a Cougar doesn't have to own something to enjoy it. He gets satisfaction from his environment on its own terms. He may sit on a fire trail, slightly troubled by the distant throb or hum of a plane whose sound has filtered down from the hillside into the canyon, or he might tighten around the eyes as he sees a ubiquitous motorcycle along the horizon. He sees and feels how out-of-place it is for wheels to be breaking the earth's skin, leaving it prey to erosion. The motorcycle is an intruder, scarring what Mother Nature has taken a thousand years to shape.

A farm labor contractor in Tulare picked up five men, including at least one Cougar, to go out to pick almonds on a San Joaquin valley ranch. When they arrived, there wasn't a tree shaker. The contractor had mallets, which he asked the men to use on the limbs so that the nuts would fall. The Cougar objected and raised a ruckus. The woman who owned the orchard came out to see what was up and seemed baffled to be told by the Cougar that you cannot treat a tree in that manner. Bruising the tree will cause sap to ooze out to heal the wound. When the cold weather comes, the tree will freeze. The five men returned to town without any money for food or a place to stay that night.

This kind of event often happens when cotton is weeded. A careless farm laborer chops a plant and is more likely to be criticized and ridiculed by fellow workers than by the labor boss. Many farm laborers cannot stand to see plants mistreated, although they are reconciled to the cutting of weeds.

"Your mention of Modesto reminded me of something I have left undone. Somebody ought to get precise information about the man or woman who started
*the* Modesto's preoccupation with lawns. We ought
*lawns* to perhaps go down together and with your help
*of* get the essential facts. I would love to write a
*Modesto* piece on *The Lawns of Modesto*, which would try to show how the example of a single man or woman can be decisive in shaping the life of a town. I am convinced that we cannot know how things happened in history unless we know who it was that made them happen."

Eric Hoffer

"You know what killed him, this great educated person? A busted appendix. He never even knew what life was.
Never knew a tree, which way the wind blows,
*getting* what a hollow bird eats. These people don't get a
*to know* chance to get outside, walk in the mountains, stay
*beauty* in the mountains, watch the mountain, see it change. No wonder they blow up. Their only release is in narcotics. It puts them in an imaginary world. I'd rather kneel down at a creek and drink out of the creek

than have a beer at any bar. And way off in the distance a bear snorts—he's got your scent—or you hear a blue jay. There's such beauty—just sit down in it and watch the clouds go by. It's a body rest, a nerve rest."

Eric Furbish

"I had been walking and hitchhiking one of California's back highways, not being very successful in getting a ride. I decided to stop and rest my sore feet. The place I picked was a lonely little canal.

"I pulled off my worn shoes and socks with the hole on the bottom of the heel, put my feet into the water, and listened to the cool flow of the dark green water. I *wounded* thought how lonely and how sad this little canal *feet* must be. Then it occurred to me that this canal and I were much alike, that we were both rambling along in a path of uncertainty, hoping to find an outlet, something along the way turning into something purposeful and meaningful, ever waiting for someone to help lift the gate that keeps us from flowing into the fields, orchards and ranch lands, in doing the work that we best know how to do.

"As I put my shoes back on, I could almost feel the true cool caressing of the water as it pressed gently against my wounded feet, as if to convey to me that it understood the very essence of my true feelings."

Kenneth Hunt

# Roaming and Goofing Off

I wanna go where there ain't no snow,
Where the sleet don't fall and the wind don't blow
In that Big Rock Candy Mountain.

Mac McClintock

Near Marysvale, Utah, are the pink and white towering alunite-quartz formations known as Big Rock Candy Mountain. Miners have been eating away at it for almost a century, and for almost as long, drifters have sung and dreamed of this mythical paradise. I remember the mid-1930s in Rock Springs, Wyoming. Early one morning I was leaving the jail, where an obliging policeman had let me spend the night, and was heading for what I thought must be the Rock Candy Mountains. I hitched rides across the desert to the Wind River range. There was great scenery, but no Big Rock Candy Mountain. I reached the wrong mountain, yet it really didn't matter to me.

For years, Cougars occasionally have asked themselves the usual whats, whys, wheres, and whens. And the questions all fade into a kind of quiet insignificance. Why does one pick up and leave? Who knows? You? Me? Hardly.

Many a Cougar has spoken of meeting someone in his life, perhaps a doughnut-shop owner or a warehouse distributor who expressed a longing for the freedom and the awareness of environment that the drifter enjoys.

"This finds me on a ranch not far from Hugo, Oklahoma. I'm feeding and branding cattle and fixing fence and all those cowboy chores that go with a ranch. Living *ride* conditions are rather primitive, but the peace of *easy* mind here is worth it. I'm alone out here with the cattle and a dog and the horses. I go to town a couple of times a month for groceries, and that's it. It's a lonely life, but I'm finding myself, and that's the important thing, isn't it. Ride easy."

Eddie Grubbs

The oceans and rivers and fields and deserts and towns and mountains are there, and you have to go and see them to be with them. They acknowledge your presence just as you acknowledge theirs. The better you understand and appreciate and go along with them, the better they treat you. It is a matter of sensing, not a matter of words.

There is the lake and the sky, and they are of you and

in you. You are part of the pulsating environment, part of the past, and now, in the present, you are keeping the faith of the land. You do not want to mistreat Mother Earth, for she brought you forth and will live on long after you have passed into her elements and vibrations.

Highways snake across the land, and if you wait patiently, some workingman or hippie will stop and take you farther along the way. He will not ask you questions that cannot be answered with words.

The railyards offer promise of new adventure. Track 1, track 2, track 3, track 4—each has a different destination.

*the boxcar vertebrae* You watch the numbering and lettering on the cars so you can tell which way is forward in the boxcar vertebrae. That long-haired brakeman nods and will even answer your question. He may even offer a suggestion or two. No longer is there the railroad bull, that sadist who would let down a rope with a piece of metal on the end that would bounce up from the ties and cut you to ribbons as you balanced yourself on the rods. But the rail life is hardly hotel-like. Pairs of human vultures prowl the yards and the boxcars for something to steal. They are ugly and mean, and they like pain—other people's pain.

One way or another you move on, sometimes walking and humming your earth songs. The wind blowing through *songs of the earth* Colorado's aspens has a special musical appeal, like the song of the cathedral pines near North Conway, New Hampshire. What wondrous water to sip in the sweet-water towns of San Andreas, Mount Shasta, Jackson, Mokulumme Hill! And the refreshing ambrosia flowing from sidewalk fountains in Salt Lake City, on the other side of the salt flats, is even better. Or you might go out of your way to try the fountain on the square in Watsonville labeled "God's Free Gift," donated by the Women's Christian Temperance Union.

You've got an urge to go to Boulder Dam and to Nogales and Tombstone and Juarez and Laredo and be part of the Mardi Gras in New Orleans. You want to see the oil platforms in the gulf of Texas and Louisiana. The Mississippi, the Mother of Rivers, as Cougars call it, gives you an uneasy feeling. You look forward to going north through the lands of your ancestors. How they ever could leave such beautiful, green country, you wonder. But your parents did leave. And so do you as you head farther north and west, noting that the lands that created the Dustbowl are planted once again. Keep the rains coming, Lord. Not another Dustbowl, please.

You travel on and on—Claremore and Muskogee, Oklahoma, and Abilene, Kansas. The White Sands and the Sangre De Cristo Mountains, Durango. Your America is not a collection of national parks and cities and towns to see. It is an America of places to be, to feel, to experience.

Your mind races with anticipation over the possibilities. Will it be a copper mine out from Tucson, the Verde River valley, or a Montana ranch this winter? Then there's the Triple J, near Ely, where they always have fences and barns to fix. Nevada is a good state. Wouldn't it be great to live out one's days near Elko? That little ad in the Western magazine said ten acres for just for $500. That's what it said. You could get part-time work if you had a spread there. Sure, just a few cattle or sheep and a vegetable garden and a few fruit trees, and you could find enough work to make ends meet. There's always someone who needs a strong back to move a piano or toss around bales of hay or sacks of grain. You like to work with your hands. You can see what you accomplish, and there are no complicated sets of instructions.

How about up to Willamette or Portland, Oregon. The day buses leave early to go out to apple-picking country. "I want to go to Washington and stay there next year, for the people are different. They treat you right, and they expect that from you, so you give it. It is altogether different," one Cougar remarked. "In May the valleys are filled with blossoms as far as the eye can see. In June there'll be the cherries and in July the apricots. In August it's the prunes, and strawberries. Then come the apples. Oh, they're delicious."

With only your near-empty wallet, knife, collapsible razor, and maybe a little spoon you've whittled, you're all set to go. No one tells you what you must do and makes you feel guilty for being what you are. You hate making mistakes, and this way you're roaming about and probably not making the mistakes that get people so uptight.

You're restless but adventurous. You want to take another swing down to the gold country, down across the Rogue River valley and on to where you can see Mount Shasta getting larger. Little wonder the Indians viewed it as a sacred mountain; it is sacred.

Oh the perfection of Whiskeytown! Why can't more towns be like that? And is the bar at LaPorte still there?

*warmth* You head for the Chiseler's Inn in Marysville. *at the* Let the rich and the immature have their Holi- *Chiseler's* day Inns and Hiltons. At the Chiseler's is warmth and good beer and an exciting blending of local history, ecology, and life in general. And they're still talking about the tourist who was so shaken when he opened the door of the fake restroom and the immodestly positioned female mannikin rose up that he slammed the door, paced around nervously, and finally handed a dollar to the waitress to give to the "nice woman" whom he thought he had offended.

You could have a gander at the new sights around Groveland and make a stop at Yosemite to see how people can flood into an area without destroying it. Humans as well as nature have done their work here on a grand scale. Cougars speak reverently of the underground "gardens" just north of Fresno and the Watts towers in the southern part of Los Angeles, those monumental achievements of single, individual, human beings.

You may feel like going to Baja, California, or back to the Snake River, the Tetons, British Columbia, and the Alcan Highway to Alaska. In a way, you're looking, not necessarily looking for something or someone, but looking—being, seeing, feeling, experiencing, growing—and saddled with the awareness that you are growing old.

> I will come, I will go
> Do not ask me why,
> For I'm just a rover
> And a passerby.
>
> chanted throughout the West—
> Source unknown

"So I'm going to take the job and go up there this summer. See what gonna happen. Money. Money is just like health. You've got it, OK; if you haven't got it, it's *it* OK, too. But I've got my health and I've got no *ain't* money, and whenever I decide to leave, I'll just *gonna* leave. Hell and high water and the wood and me *bother* and the works, I'll just go. That's me. So I'll see *me* what I can do here; it really looks prosperous. I like it anyway and I like the people and I like the place, and I like the work. Lloyd thinks I might just get skinned out of my loot, but I don't think I will. But if I do, it ain't gonna bother me, but it may bother just plumb hell out of the other people, first trying, thinking they skin me. So they skin me, so what. Let the old dog sleep, don't keep kicking him."

A Cougar describing his wandering ways.

A bookish Cougar who works the ships wrote me: "For a long time I kidded myself that the crass commercialism of man-woman companionship as evidenced in the Far East was nonexistent for me. I seldom directly parted with cold cash for favors. Still money was never in my pockets long enough to discolor them. The dozen odd trips that I took into the Phillipine hinterland, while inexpensive by U.S. mode of travel, mounted up in costs when two were involved. I have no regrets, however. A guide was always necessary, for once away from the waterfront, the sound of English was seldom heard. Long ago I discovered that bar girls, while reconciled to their lives, nevertheless were never unwilling to leave their environment for a day or two or for a week at far less pay, there being undoubtedly less wear and tear. The same was true both in Taiwan and in Japan. I've probably done far more traveling than the average merchant seaman and have earned the dubious honor of being called a 'scenery bum.'

*scenery bum*

"Yet I long for the camaraderie of the sea and of the men who sail on it, of the ships of every nation, of the multitude of friends that I have met, and of the anticipation of seeing them once again; especially in Japan. I wish that I had some particular talent that could be put to use over there for I should really like to live there, not for always perhaps. But long enough to be able to speak the language, and to learn to know the people better. The politest and friendliest people that I have ever met."

•          •          •

"We were in the spargus. Bill gave me a crew of thirty men, and so I had thirty men. Had about twelve fellers, white fellers. I called them old seagulls. They *in* were good cutters. And I had quite a few Mexican *the* fellers, and quite a few colored fellers. And I had *spargus* four or five younger white guys. They'd work a day and quit. All they wanted was enough money to get a bottle of wine. Now that's the truth. They're winos. Any joker drinks wine, he's off my list. I don't care if they sip or guzzle it, if they can't find something else to drink. I'd rather drink horse piss. Anyway, anybody who drinks that stuff ain't got a good head on them. Good wine, OK, but that wino cheap crap, no way. Anyway, I worked there for two or three weeks, I don't know, but the spargus were real good, and I was kind of a shift boss. I had my men and had 'em going fine.

"I'm the one who messed this up. I knew another feller was a foreman on another crew. We had three crews. So I *wound* had a few checks in my pocket, and it was Satur- *up in* day night and we all went into El Centro for a *Mexicali* few beers, and you guessed it. It wasn't long be- fore we wound up in Mexicali. And, well, I met a nice pretty little señorita and forgot to come home. I was gone three days. Well, too bad, no work down there. Life would have been altogether different today. Had to come back up here where the jobs are. No work down there. And so I lost my foreman job. Bill wasn't mad, but he was sure disgusted. And spargus left off there and I come back up here to work. . . ."

•          •          •

"Then there was old Perry Daniel. A good guy, a chopper. And him and I tried to get out of work one day. He was falling, and I was bucking up. It was raining and *soppin* the wind was blowing, so we told the foreman that *wet in* we didn't want to come to work. So it was all right *Myrtle* with him. We got back in Perry's jeep and headed *Creek* for home. Well, we went by Myrtle Creek. Myrtle Creek's got a few colors of gold in it so we jumps out. It was pouring rain and we jumps out to see what was going on down at the creek, panning through gravel and stuff like that and getting sopping wet, right to the skin, sopping wet. And there we were down there looking, and we got nothing and yet we spent all that time in that creek, enjoying ourselves. Didn't make a damn penny, and we could've gone up there and felled timber and bucked up the logs and made real good money. Boy, what fools we are sometimes.

"Another time Perry and me—he sung in the choir in church, you wouldn't believe it though—so, we wanted a salmon or two, so we got gaff hooks and went on up where they were getting ready to spawn. Well, that's a misdemeanor, or at least there's quite a penalty if they catch you. Where the water was shallow, we saw some backs sticking out. I pitched a rock and hit one, and it was soon belly-up floating downstream. I was really surprised. I hollered, 'I hit him, I hit him!' That's pretty good. I'll never be able to do it again the rest of my life. Got to thinking about that fish though. But holy smokes, that was really something.!

"But Perry, you know, on Sunday, just like an angel, got up in the choir and sang tenor. You'd never think that he'd grab a gaff hook after choir and go up to the spawning grounds."

●     ●     ●

"We'd get paid every two weeks. We'd have a real blowout. So, we were coming back to work one Sunday, get- *when ya* ting ready to come back to work on Monday, it *gotta* was. Red, he and I stopped into the last bar, the *go* Sportsman. Red liked Jim Beam, so he asks the bartender for a bottle of Jim Beam. Well, the fellow must not of understood him right. He gave him a bottle of gin, but Red didn't know it. The guy put it in a paper bag, wrapped it, and Red paid for it, and we finished up and started on down the street, hitchhiking along the highway to the Smith River. That's fourteen miles to Crescent City. Got a ride. Then when we got out Red had to go off into the brush. That's down from the highway, so I just walked slow waiting for him. And all at once down in there, I heard a real gasping sound, really gasping. Turned around and Red had ahold of his throat. His face was red like he was being hung by a rope. Couldn't get his breath. And in his other hand he had that paper bag with the neck of the bottle sticking out of it. And it was about a quarter of a minute 'til he got a little breath, and I asked him what's wrong down there. I thought he was having some kind of seizure. He says, 'Ah the sonofabitch, he gave me a bottle of gin instead of Jim Beam. Guy must have thought I said gin instead of Jim.' He was a-coughin' and a-sneezin' and a-chokin'. He was something else that guy. Comical. Just to look at him you had to laugh. . . ."

•       •       •

"At this Morning Mine they gave room and board, and did we eat. We ate like kings, better than kings in fact. . . .

On the table, for instance, the drinks alone—there

*we ate* were coffee, tea, icewater with ice, milk, butter-
*like* milk, just cold water and a soft drink. For meats—
*kings* chops, roasts, pork chops—you name it, it was
there, along with the rest of the supper, such as vegetables and such like that. It was pretty good.

"Breakfast, when you came down, the waitress asked you what you wanted and how much and how you wanted it. I would ask for five eggs scrambled in cream, three hot cakes, milk, coffee, butter, and a hunk of ham. And it was a hunk. Oh boy, how the American Smelting Company did feed in those days!

"For your room, it's like a hotel with a shower, except for the dry. The dry was where we changed from our diggers to our street clothes. Everybody had his own separate room, unless you had a buddy. Then they gave you a room with twin beds in it. Me, I had no such one, for I had left my so-called good buddy, that girl back in the coal-mine country with a frothing husband, fit to shoot me.

"Her and I were planning on leaving, just about the time he found out, and her stuff was all in my suitcases. I

*one of* had thrown all my clothes out and put all her
*these* clothes in my suitcases. Then I left in a hurry,
*days* checked into Greyhound, got me a ticket, and got
*I'll find* on that bus to Wallace, Idaho, and took off.
*her* When I got to the mine where I was staying, I
opened up the suitcases and what did I see but

all women's clothes. Not a stitch was there for me. I had
forgotten all about her stuff being in my suitcases. Some
shock did I have. Oh well, love is sure grand. And I have
had a lot of grand, with love spread on, quite thin at times. I
won't stop looking even if I live to be a hundred. One of
these days I'll find her, and if I don't, well, such is life. Oh
well, I've had a lot of fun looking anyway."

Eric Furbish

# The Endangered Species

To me, tomorrow never comes, for when it's here, it's today. . . . I guess I'm restless, looking for something that I haven't found. I can't exactly tell what I'm looking for, but feel sure that I'll know when I find it. Of course I may die before I do.

Louis "Luke" Miller

I just live life.

A Cougar Refrain

The youth in me is not all there anymore, but what's

left I'm doing all I can with it.
                              Charles "Slim" Rodgers

It's currently popular to be deeply concerned about one or another species of endangered animal. Magazines carry features, newspapers print letters, organizations vote resolutions, and societies are founded to protect one or another rare animal. Among the convincing arguments is that each species is important to the total world environment. Conditions on our earth are changing. The composition of the skies and seas is changing so much that dire predictions about the very survival of life on our planet are common in many quarters.

"Experts" point out that changes in the adaptability of species may be of crucial importance to the survival of other, seemingly unrelated species. But who is to say what kinds of life will provide us with clues to human survival?

Could it not be that different traits and personality types might play this same role? How about the individualist who can adjust to any noninstitutional, nonsymbolic living arrangement, who is willing to work without asking, "What's in it for me?" who doesn't try living in the past or in some unborn future? Might this not be an adaptable species that will help the human race to survive when the skies and the cities and the land are chemically and thermally out of balance? Consider for a moment. If you were stranded on a remote desert island tomorrow with but one other person, would you rather that person be a professor of medieval history or a Cougar?

As a loner, the Cougar doesn't have an organization or a lobby to protect his interests. No one speaks up for him. Without any membership affiliations and with a live-and-let-live philosophy, he doesn't seem to fit into our highly structured, institutionalized modern society. He remains quiet as city and county planners destroy his environment.

Regrettably, the human Cougar is on the way to extinction. He is truly an endangered species.

The Cougar usually recognizes that he is out of step with civilization's institutions. One of them, Louis "Luke" Miller, told me the following: "I was in the Santa Monica bus station, and right in broad daylight this young dude walked over and grabbed the purse of a woman about sixty. She had it over her forearm and, holding on, was pulled down to the floor. No one close to her did anything, and I ran over and whomped this dude. After a minute or so of fighting, I had his arms held so he couldn't get away.

"Well, soon the police arrived, and the police wanted to arrest me, too. The woman and a couple bystanders spoke up and said I had helped her keep her purse, but the police took both the dude and me off to jail anyhow.

"I was sitting there the next morning when the lock-key came up and said I was bailed out by the woman. I went to her house to thank her, and she let me do a couple days of painting. Well, in about two weeks, the case came to court. The judge told me I was charged with "vicious assault." The woman jumped up and shouted that I had just been helping her, and I shouldn't be held for that. Believe it or not, but the judge told her to be quiet or he would hold her for being in contempt of court. After this, I was almost surprised to get off. You figure it out. I don't understand it. It's a kind of jungle."

In addition to not having any club affiliation except something like a temporary union card for temporary work purposes, the Cougar is self-contained. He accepts responsibility for his own life and the ways of his life. He sees himself as having created his own patterns of living; he does not blame family, childhood upbringing, wives or girl friends, the economic system, or other people for his misfortunes. If drinking is a problem, and somehow this seems to be frequently the case with the older Cougar, he believes that he drinks because he wants to and that he wants to drink because of some associational situation—perhaps just to fill up time.

We have seen that the Cougar's history has been one of drifting, doing the necessary work at the times and places where the West was opening up agricultural, forest, and mining areas. When the levee had to be built (and later sandbagged to save a town), when a mine needed another drift to be able to stay in business, when wood was required, when a raging forest fire had to be stopped, when crops had to be harvested, or when cattle had to be taken to the market—all tasks that were short-term but vital to the existence of the West—there you would find the Cougar, working in spurts, often at hard physical labor or at work requiring ingenuity instead of expensive machines to do the job. This work required special talents and dispositions. To some extent, this pattern is still true.

Without ownership of any of the bases of production or processes of distribution, with no chance for economic gain beyond the week's pay, the Cougar does what needs to be done. For a while he makes it his own and then moves on when the project is completed. He doesn't wait around until he can qualify for county or state or federal welfare; he doesn't wait for the mine to reopen six months later; he doesn't wait for the next fishing season. As his own man with his own self-respect, he temporarily holes up in some skid-row or workingman's hotel, or in a camp, cave, or jungle. When he gets restless, he heads into his next experience by taking a freight car or Greyhound or by hitching a ride or maybe by walking.

Sometimes he can still meet a girl with whom a relationship lasting several months or even years becomes possible, but his drifting ways, his lack of any stable, long-term employment or welfare, and his lack of seniority make it hard for married or common-law living. The woman needs something more, something different, particularly for the sake of the children. The Cougar finds himself an outsider, unable to sit before the hearth.

As automation of agricultural work accelerates and as more and more farm labor contractors come from minority groups and favor those of their own racial and social origins, the Cougar finds his services in agriculture and ranching usable for only a few months of the year at most. He can stay at farm labor camps, dirty as they are, and when he does tolerate them, he finds it tempting to go along on the wine and become partially oblivious, at least for a little while, to his surroundings.

With no real training or skill, often with a major defect —perhaps the loss of an eye in a logging accident (it had never occurred to him to demand compensation for his injury)—with no work references, and with age catching up, he has few job opportunities. If he has a record, even though the arrests are mostly for drinking, the Cougar is likely to be shunned as an undesirable. Why risk hiring someone who may wander off the job at any time or for whom all kinds of liability claims and Social Security might feasibly have to be paid? It is better to rely on the ambitious young, the "home guard" and others who are trying to get ahead. The Cougar knows this and after many rebuffs goes along his solitary way, glad for the good fortune of others and only a little apprehensive about his own future. He knows that if he keeps moving he will keep ahead of the blues. He has seen those who drink in bed; they are the ones who die first.

When the moving-on becomes tougher, as the jobs become more scarce, and when you discover aches and pains in hitherto unnoticed places and tendons and sinews appear where you had only been aware of flesh and muscle, you pause long enough to have an extra beer, or two, or three and maybe ask for the first time, "where am I going?"

That is when the dream begins to take shape. Usually, it concerns an acre or plot on the edge of a town, somewhere in the foothills of the Sierra Nevada, in the great central valleys of California, in the backlands of Colorado, Montana, Oregon, Idaho, or Utah. You picture yourself retaining your freedom, raising most of the food you need and storing it for winter, working part-time on ranches, and doing a little gold prospecting. You figure out how you could heat a small mobile trailer with a wood-burner and how you can fish in some nearby stream or lake. You have this dream of settling down for once, though basically remaining independent. Sometimes it does happen, but more often than not, the dream is cut short by the onslaught of ill health, the coughing of blood, rapid physical deterioration caused by old injuries, years of overexposure, excessive smoking, and undisciplined eating and drinking.

In 1968 five Cougars met with my wife and me to share their lives and outlooks. For two days we discussed the life of the Cougar and the possibility of mutual help. There was general awareness that this was a get-together of the unorganizable trying to organize. Not a single Cougar knew how to make the compromises necessary to organize formally. Nonetheless, "Rules of the Cougars, Inc." was drawn up by the meeting's elected president, O. Lloyd Hicks.

## RULES OF THE COUGARS, INC.

1. Be a gentleman, fair and honest at all times, always looking forward to helping other Cougars and also other people.

2. Pass the goals of the Cougars on to other people, so they will understand what we are striving to do.

3. Work at losing all greed within ourselves and really help other Cougars to the kind of life they desire in their future years.

4. For some, a little improvement is better than none at all, because a Cougar has many good traits and is a high-type individual, but he has been sliding his wheels trying to get a firm hold on the future.

5. Really take a good personal inventory of one's self, and list the good and bad. We try to improve or fulfill the need of our faults with something good and constructive.

6. Be willing to work with other social groups and organizations for the welfare and future of the Cougars and other humans.

7. Be sincere in our daily, positive actions, and try to preserve the true meaning and cause of the Cougars.

8. Preserve our independent way without personal downfall.

9. As we get going and have more or less found our adjustment for the future, contribute to the Cougar treasury, so we can carry on and help others, as there are many.

10. We all know it takes time and money for this cause, so we all have our obligation to help with funds to make this organization grow and help our future Cougars.

11. Money will be disbursed by the treasurer, presi-

dent, and one other member after they have agreed to its worthy use.

12. The Cougar name shall be used for the express purpose of the Cougars themselves and used only with the agreement of the president, secretary, and one other member.

13. As one Cougar to another, we will work together for the benefit of all. All suggestions will be considered by the board, and useful ones will be used to the advantage of the Cougars.

14. Carry out our ideals regardless of whatever roadblocks seem to appear. It's much easier to solve a problem with a group of Cougars than as individuals.

15. Remember our positions in the past and wasted days and years. It will take time to gain our objectives—slow and easy—but for sure.

16. We don't blame anyone else, family, other people, government, for our present circumstances.

17. We are older now, tired of our adventurous travels, and want to knuckle down but still have an independent way to help others and the young.

That was the first and last planned get-together of the Cougars.

Inasmuch as the Cougars are not likely to ensure their own survival, it will depend upon the rest of us, particularly those who understand and appreciate the unique part they continue to have in our national heritage and civilization.

I have known individuals high in industry, engineering, mining, building and craft trades, and many walks of life who had strong Cougar strains and refused to be straitjacketed by their work. These have included both men and women, ranging in age from their teens into their nineties. I have also met several Cougarish individuals with large, inherited financial resources or "windfalls" from inventions or ideas who live in some measure of splendid isolation. It has been interesting to see how those with a Cougar strain—courageous, resourceful, independent, and with directness of insight—generally are at first startled and then respond favorably when they meet a mature Human Cougar face-to-face.

It is these persons with a Cougar strain who will probably determine the survival of the Cougar species. Whether it might have any bearing on the ultimate survival of humanity itself will not be known in our lifetime.